PIVOT POINT

PIVOT POINT FUNDAMENTALS: COSMETOLOGY
COLOR

©1980-2021 Pivot Point International, Inc.
All rights reserved.
ISBN 978-1-940593-48-7

1st Edition
4th Printing, October 2021
Printed in China

Pivot Point International, Inc.
Global Headquarters
8725 West Higgins Road, Suite 700
Chicago, IL 60631 USA

847-866-0500
pivot-point.com

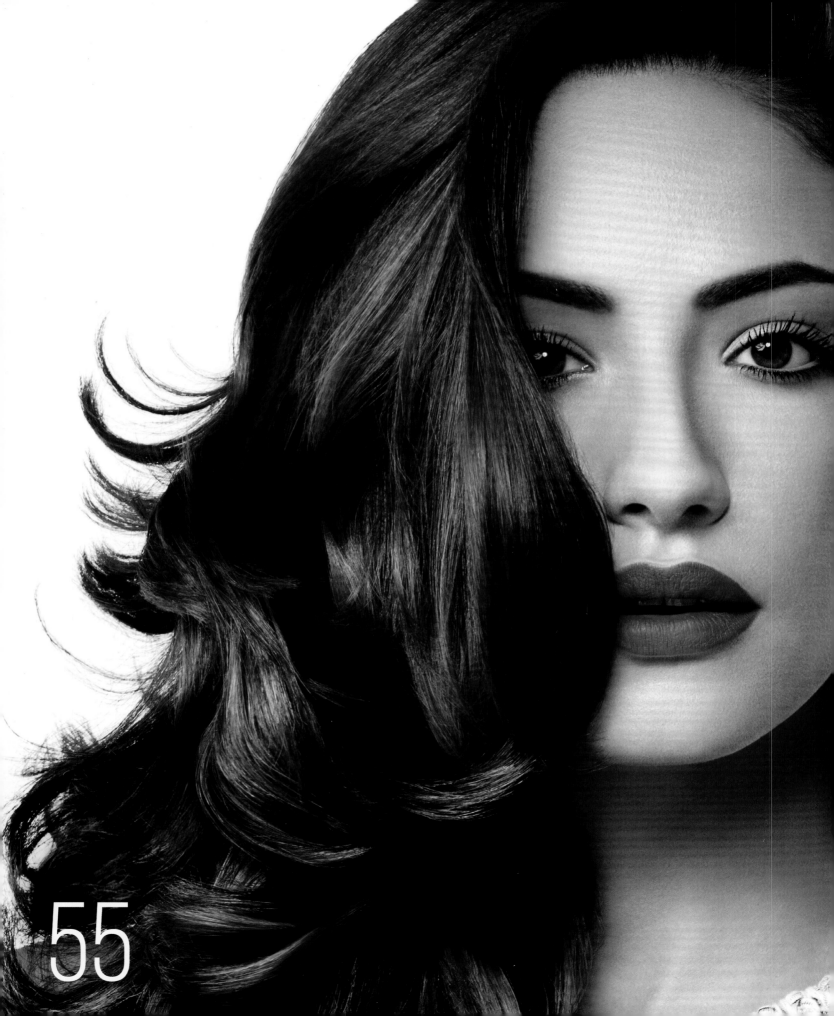

110c // COLOR
CONTENTS

98

44

2

81

81

32

18

2

18

44

98

115

115

73

COLOR APPLICATOR

110ᶜ.1 //
COLOR THEORY

EXPLORE //

When choosing a color product from store shelves, besides the picture on the product, how would you know what the color would look like on your hair?

Mathias Appel

INSPIRE //

Learning and understanding color theory will give you the foundation to create endless color possibilities and solve some of the biggest color challenges you might encounter in your career.

ACHIEVE //

Following this lesson on *Color Theory,* you'll be able to:

>> Restate in your own words the law of color

>> Identify the three primary colors and explain how they are used to create secondary and tertiary colors

>> Distinguish the characteristics of color, including hue, value and intensity

FOCUS //

COLOR THEORY

The Law of Color

Color Wheel

Warm and Cool Colors

Complementary Colors

Characteristics of Color

In today's salons, color services are such an important part of the business that many designers choose to specialize in color. Understanding the foundation for hair coloring is just as important as the application techniques themselves. Whether you choose to use shades that range from soft and natural, to bold and bright, a thorough understanding of how color works in relation to the hair you're applying it to, is key to your success. It will provide you with unlimited creative expression when designing color for your clients.

Every once in a while, you might encounter a client who's had a bad hair color experience, either due to home coloring or the work of another stylist—maybe you! When fixing mishaps, your thorough understanding of the color principles in this lesson will be critical in the color correction. Making these clients feel good again will gain you not only their appreciation but also their loyalty and referrals.

Hair coloring techniques have been used since ancient times. Cleopatra was said to have used henna to add reddish tones. Roman women used mixtures of wood ash, unslaked lime and sodium bicarbonate to lighten their hair. In the mid-1800s a German professor, August Wilhelm von Hofmann, and one of his students, William Henry Perkin, accidentally discovered how to create permanent dyes. Their discovery led to the synthetic hair colorants that are used today, which change color in one of two ways:

1. Temporarily: By adding color pigment that shampoos out (immediately or over time)

2. Permanently: Either by adding or removing color pigment

Color is the visual perception of the reflection of light. Without light there would be no color. In other words, color is a phenomenon of light. Sir Isaac Newton discovered this fact in 1676 when he passed white light through a prism and found that the light broke out into continuous bands of color, ranging from red to orange to yellow, then green to blue to indigo and finally violet.

Each of these colors is a group of electromagnetic waves, also called wavelengths, traveling through space. Those not visible to the eye include:

» Radio waves
» Infrared waves

Wavelengths that can be seen create color and are known as "visible light." Wavelengths cannot be seen unless they are reflected off an object. The brain interprets these waves of light as color. For example, when white light shines on a red object, the object absorbs most of the light waves except the red ones. The reflected red light waves are interpreted by the eye as the color red.

VISIBLE AND INVISIBLE LIGHT

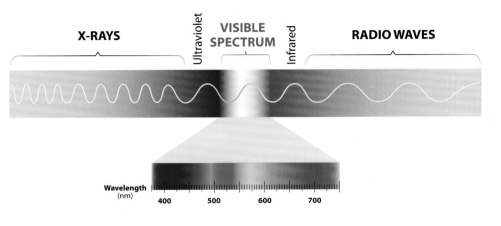

THE LAW OF COLOR

The law of color states that only three colors—yellow, red and blue, called primary colors—are "pure" colors, meaning they cannot be created by mixing together any other colors. The three primary colors create all the other colors.

When two of the three primary colors are mixed in varying proportions, they produce the three secondary colors:

>> **Orange:** Contains varying proportions of red and yellow

>> **Green:** Contains varying proportions of blue and yellow

>> **Violet:** Contains varying proportions of red and blue

Mixing a primary color with its neighboring secondary color in varying proportions makes tertiary colors. The six tertiary colors are:

>> Yellow-orange

>> Red-orange

>> Red-violet

>> Blue-violet

>> Blue-green

>> Yellow-green

PRIMARY COLORS

Yellow   *Red*   *Blue*

SECONDARY COLORS

Orange   *Green*   *Violet*

TERTIARY COLORS

Yellow-Orange   *Red-Orange*   *Red-Violet*

Blue-Violet   *Blue-Green*   *Yellow-Green*

COLOR WHEEL

A color wheel is a 12-hue color circle that is created from the three primary colors, which then are used to create the three secondary and six tertiary colors, positioned in a circle, allowing any mixed color to be described in relation to the primary colors. **The name of a color, also referred to as tone or hue, is identified by its position on the wheel. The tone of a hair color can be described as warm, cool or neutral.**

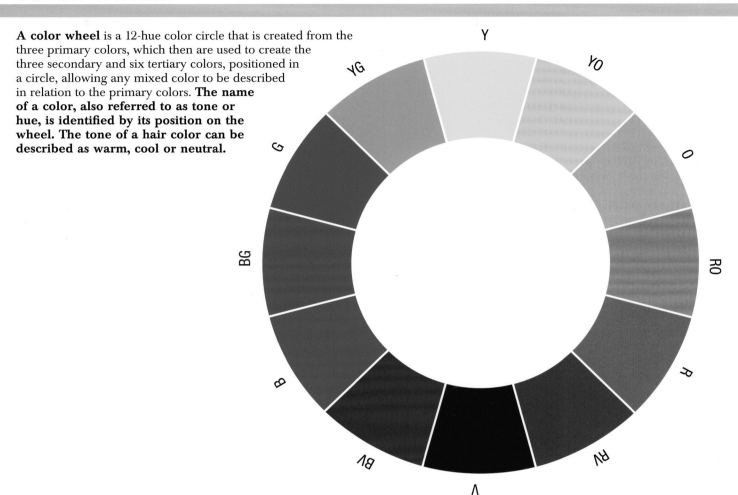

Color Wheel

Create your own color wheel with white yak hair and nonoxidative colors so you can experience the law of color first-hand.

Be aware that color pigmentation from one hair color manufacturer to another varies slightly, so get familiar, and test the color line you're working with.

As an alternative, you could also use food coloring in water or Play-Doh.

WARM AND COOL COLORS

Colors can be classified as either warm colors (warm tones) or cool colors (cool tones).

» **Warm color tones** generally fall into the yellow, orange or red half of the color wheel.

» **Cool color tones** generally fall into the green, blue and violet half of the color wheel.

» Yellow-green and violet-red can be considered warm or cool, depending on whether they contain more of the cool tones or warm tones.

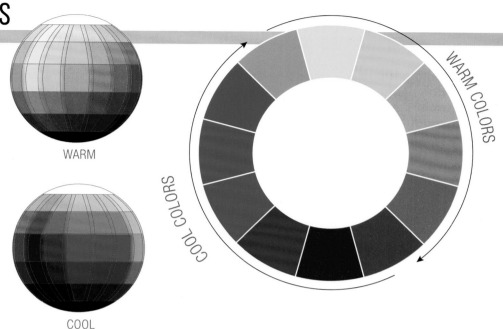

WARM

COOL

WARM COLORS

COOL COLORS

Any colored object or substance can be categorized as warm or cool, even people—based on their hair and skin tones. **If someone is classified as warm, this means their hair and skin coloring fall into the yellow, red and orange category,** or in other words, has those undertones.

SALON**CONNECTION**

How can you tell if a client has warm or cool undertones? If you turn their wrist over, blue veins equal cool undertones, green veins equal warm undertones, and a combination of both means neutral.

COMPLEMENTARY COLORS

Colors found opposite one another on the color wheel are referred to as complementary colors. When two complementary colors are combined, the result contains all three primary colors. When complementary colors are mixed together in varying proportions, they neutralize or cancel one another out, eventually producing a neutral color, such as certain shades of gray, black or brown, depending on the proportions used. Colors that do not exhibit warm or cool tones are considered neutral colors.

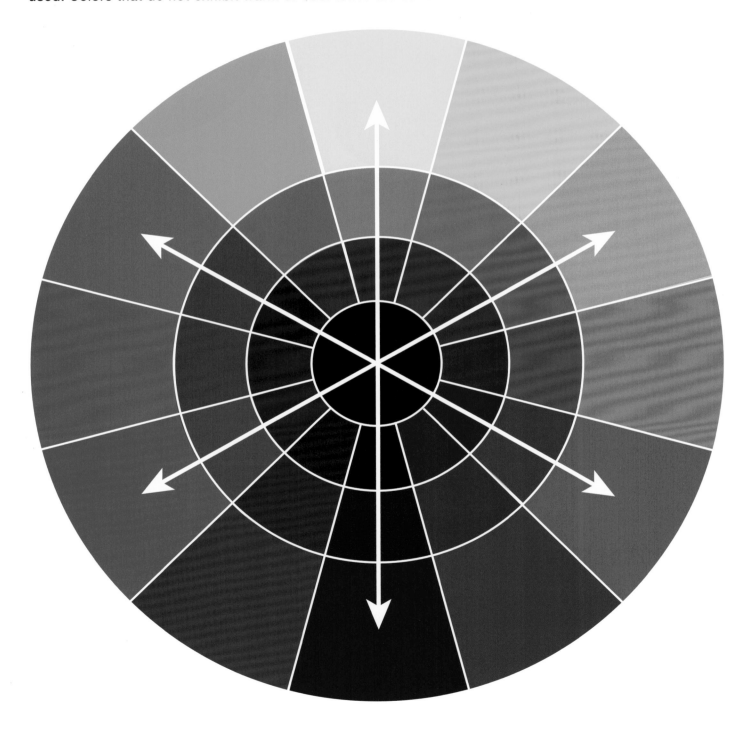

Complementary colors are often used to correct or neutralize unwanted tones. For instance, a client's hair may have lightened to a brassy, orange tone. A correction is possible by using the color wheel to determine that blue is the complementary color to orange and, therefore, applying a blue-based color to the brassy tone will neutralize or correct it to achieve the desired final shade.

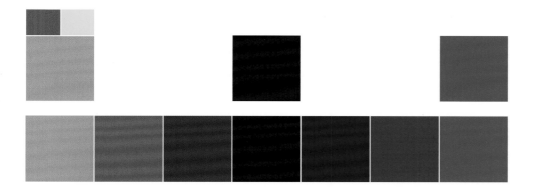

Varying proportions of the three primary colors create a range of brown and/or neutral colors.

Light golden brown contains more yellow.

Medium reddish-brown contains more red.

Neutral brown contains more blue.

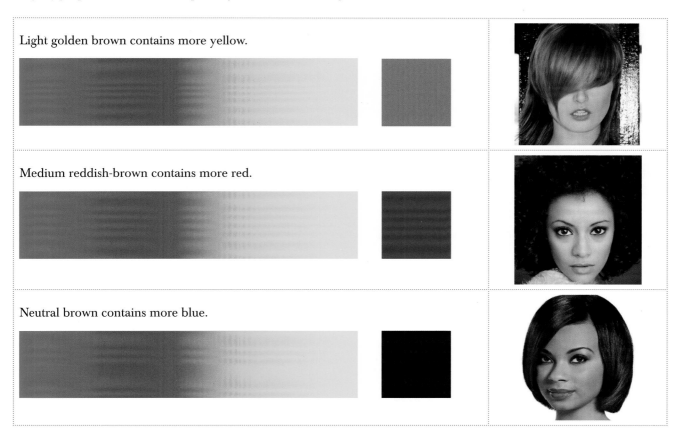

CHARACTERISTICS OF COLOR

Color has three main characteristics:

>> Hue
>> Level/Value
>> Intensity

The characteristics of hue, level/value and intensity are used to describe all color products you'll encounter in the salon.

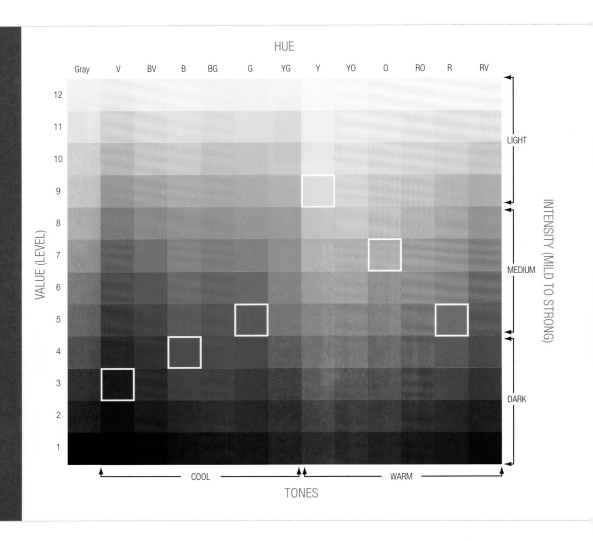

HUE

Hues are named and abbreviated for easy reference based on their position on the color wheel. These abbreviations are often used by manufacturers to identify the specific hues of hair coloring products.

>> Primary and secondary colors are all abbreviated by their first initial
  ■ Y for yellow
  ■ R for red
  ■ B for blue
  ■ G for green
  ■ O for orange
  ■ V for violet

>> Names of the six tertiary colors are combinations of the primary and secondary color, for example:
  ■ RO for red-orange
  ■ BV for blue-violet

LEVEL/VALUE

The color level, also referred to as its value, is the degree of lightness or darkness of a color, relative to itself and to other colors.

» Yellow is described as a light color.
» Red is described as a medium color.
» Blue is described as a dark color.

There are two ways that hair colorists talk about the value of hair colors: fields and levels. All hair colors in the world can be categorized into three major fields:

» **Light**
» **Medium**
» **Dark**

The fields can be further subdivided into medium dark and medium light.

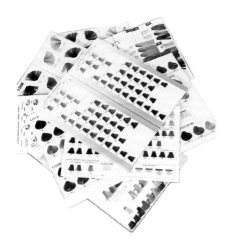

The level system is a numbering system that identifies the lightness or darkness of hair colors in smaller specific increments.

Both natural and artificial hair color is divided into 10 numbered levels:

» Darkest hair color is level 1

» Lightest hair color is level 10

» Some manufacturers use a 1-12 level system that operates the same way. In this instance 12 is the lightest color.

DISCOVER**MORE**

Search online for different hair color charts to see how these levels are applied.

You can further understand level by thinking of a photo with a black and white filter put on it. You see the photo in various shades of gray, which represent the relative lightness or darkness of the colors in the photo. Once you add color back to the photo, the color levels won't change.

Note how lighter colors seem to come forward and darker colors seem to recede.

Hair colorists use value and levels to classify hair color as light, medium or dark when measured against a gray scale. Consider if and where lightness/darkness should be positioned in a style to create added depth, dimension or textural interest. Then, visualize your design in hues of color.

INTENSITY

Intensity refers to the vividness, brightness or saturation of a color within its own level. The intensity of a color can range from mild to strong. Words used to describe the intensity of a color include:

>> Strong intensity – Deep, vibrant, rich

>> Soft intensity – Subtle, muted, soft

Intensity describes the strength of a color's tone, not its lightness or darkenss. The most intense version of a color is sometimes referred to as "pure" because it represents the most saturated version of that color.

You can use characteristics of a color chart to identify the intensity of colors and how the intensity relates to the value. This relates back to what you learned about primary colors, fields of colors and the level system. Primary colors, in their purest intensity, vary in level, with **pure blue being the darkest of the three primary colors**.

>> Yellow is lightest

>> Red is medium

>> **Blue is darkest**

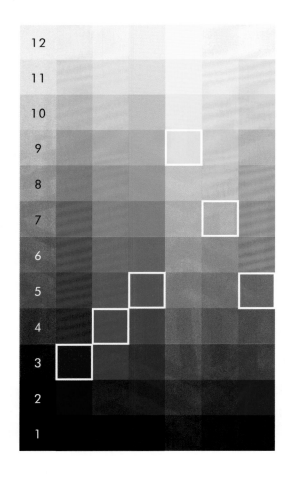

Understanding and appropriately applying color theory will help you create beautiful color designs for your clients, as well as correct any color mishaps.

LESSONS LEARNED

>> The law of color states that yellow, red and blue are "pure" colors that can't be created by mixing together any other colors.

>> When two of the three primary colors are mixed in varying proportions, they produce the secondary colors:

- Orange
- Green
- Violet

Mixing a primary color with its neighboring secondary color makes tertiary colors:

- Yellow-orange
- Red-orange
- Red-violet
- Blue-violet
- Blue-green
- Yellow-green

>> Characteristics of color include:

- Hue – Identified and named by its position on the color wheel

- Level/Value – The degree of lightness or darkness of a color, ranging from 1-10 or 1-12

- Intensity – The brightness or vividness of a color

110ᶜ.2
COLOR DESIGN

INSPIRE //

Understanding the relationship between visualizing your color design and where to place color is one of the most important aspects of designing your color transformations and will provide you with unlimited creative expressions for your clients.

EXPLORE //

With the broad variety of hair color products available at the drugstore, how can you make sure the results of your color services are superior to those a client can achieve at home?

ACHIEVE //

Following this lesson on *Color Design,* you'll be able to:

≫ Identify the effects color can have on overall design

≫ Describe the visual changes of the form and texture of a style when the hair color is changed

≫ Analyze hair color on basic, detailed and abstract levels of observation

≫ Summarize a series of design decisions that will lead to the desired color design result

FOCUS //

COLOR DESIGN

Color Design Transformation

Color Design Analysis

Color Design Decisions

Change the Color, Change the Effect

110ᶜ.2 | COLOR DESIGN

Color can define the lines and shape of a hair design, soften facial features, warm skin tones and accentuate a person's lifestyle and personality. Dispersed throughout a design, color can unify contrasting elements. It may be a background element, visually leading the viewer's eye to a focal area, or it may be the element that actually creates the focal point.

Trained designers help guide their hair color clients by listening to their concerns and offering suggestions. They also bring the available color selections into focus by discussing color placement and patterns that will be beneficial for the client's overall hairstyle and texture. It takes careful consideration, a trained eye and a well-planned set of procedural steps to create successful color designs time after time.

COLOR DESIGN TRANSFORMATION

Specific reasons why clients decide to color their hair are just as abundant as the variety of colors available to you as a stylist. Some of the more common motivations for a color change include:

TO CREATE A FASHION STATEMENT

TO ENHANCE EXISTING OR NATURAL HAIR COLOR

TO COVER OR BLEND GRAY

TO MIMIC OR CORRECT THE SUN'S LIGHTENING EFFECTS

Color transformation is not only about changing the shade of a hair color, but also about patterns and placement of color. Based on the patterns and color placement you choose, you can:

» Visually change or enhance the form of a design

» Visually change or enhance the texture of a design

» Create a focal point while leading the eye through a design

EFFECTS OF COLOR ON FORM

A repetition of one color throughout, as well as strategic placement of darker colors, draw attention away from the texture and focus on the form or silhouette.

An all-over application of a darker color draws attention to the overall form of a design.

Placing darker colors in close-fitting areas and lighter colors where more expansion is desired can enhance the form of the design.

EFFECTS OF COLOR ON TEXTURE

The texture of a design can be either emphasized or de-emphasized based on the color patterns and the degree of difference between the colors chosen.

A repetition of color can visually calm an otherwise activated texture.

An alternation in a selected area can accentuate the sculpted texture.

EFFECTS OF COLOR AS A FOCAL POINT

Selective placement can create a focal point or accentuate a focal point that was created during another service, such as a sculpture or hair design.

A darker color at the nape visually narrows the head shape, while a transition of lighter blonds toward the face creates softness.

A soft fusion of warm colors through the mid-lengths and ends gives the appearance of more movement and dimension.

A dark shadow with a bright accent color that frames the face creates a dynamic focal point that emphasizes the eyes and geometric fringe.

Lighter accents in the interior of an overall darker design can draw attention and emphasize the interior lengths.

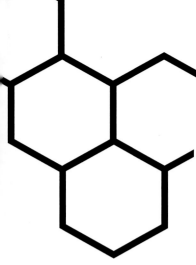

COLOR DESIGN ANALYSIS

Color designing is part of a total composition, which also includes the other design elements of form and texture. Designing color includes identifying:

» Existing and desired color
» Patterns, shapes and techniques that will be used

Thorough client consultation is of utmost importance to ensure that you'll produce what the client has in mind.

When creating color designs, it's about more than choosing a color and applying it to the hair—it starts with analyzing a color design like a designer would, breaking it down using the three levels of observation:

» Basic
» Detail
» Abstract

BASIC

Look at the color design and identify if what you see is:

» Light
» Medium
» Dark
» Same color throughout
» Patterns of colors

Visualizing in black and white will help determine the lightness or darkness.

DETAIL

Look closer to identify the color(s) based on:

» Hair color family
» Warmth or coolness
» Intensity
» Whether it is a light, warm brown or a medium, cool brown

Remember the characteristics of color you studied in *Color Theory*.

ABSTRACT

Imagine the placement of color to create the effects you see.

A color graphic is a representation of the color scheme that identifies:

» Placement of color(s)
» Patterns and shapes used

COLOR DESIGN DECISIONS

When designing unique hair colors, be guided by what you learn during your client consultation. Also be inspired by the sculpted form, the existing as well as the desired color, and flattering color shades and tones. Explore how you want to alter or emphasize the existing form and texture or whether the color should create a focal area.

SCULPTED FORM

The sculpted form serves as an inspiration for color placement and patterns. The examples below illustrate how color can be used to emphasize or de-emphasize the classic shape and texture characteristics of the four basic forms.

SOLID FORM //

Deeper tones at the perimeter enhance the form line and add visual weight.

Highlights around the face create a focal point.

Highlights throughout create the illusion of surface activation and more movement.

GRADUATED FORM //

Darker tones in the exterior enhance the tapered effect and angular shape of the nape.

Interior highlights create a more activated appearance to balance the sculpted activated texture in the exterior.

A repetition of color throughout diminishes the contrast of the sculpted textures and draws attention to the shape of the form.

INCREASE-LAYERED FORM //

Lighter ends showcase activated texture and the elongation of the form.

Lighter tones in the interior create the illusion of more volume.

All-over highlights increase the illusion of texture activation, particularly on the long interior layers.

UNIFORMLY LAYERED FORM //

A repetition of color throughout enhances the shape of the form.

Highlights near the face create a focal point.

An alternation of color throughout adds to the appearance of texture activation.

| DARK | MEDIUM | LIGHT |

EXISTING/DESIRED LEVEL

Identifying the existing and desired levels can be an easy way to think about color placement before thinking about the many shades in color design. Remember that dark colors visually recede and emphasize shape and shine, while lighter colors stand out, create the illusion of more volume and allow more texture detail to be seen. So, be intentional when you decide where to position lights and/or darks.

Color design transformations begin with looking at color options as they relate to lightness or darkness of the color. Afterwards, you'll want to observe and think about shade or tonality.

Questions to guide you include:

» Should I go lighter or darker, or stay in the same level and just add tone?

» Should I create textural interest by breaking up the light reflection with an alternation of light and dark colors?

» Should I create a dramatic effect using contrasting levels of colors?

SALON**CONNECTION**

"Hard to Tell"

Critical in the consultation process is determining what areas you want to emphasize or de-emphasize. Ask open-ended questions to find out what your client is looking for, for example: "How happy are you with your hair color?" You'll be surprised to find that the vast majority of clients will tell you something that they wish were different. Remember, every color design should serve a purpose beyond its shade or covering gray hair, whether it is to create shine and showcase the haircut, create softness, or create a focal point. If the client is having a hard time answering, ask what she *doesn't* like about her color. Oftentimes people have an easier time identifying what they don't like versus what they do like.

COLOR PLACEMENT

Creating hair colors with specially designed placement is a sure way of differentiating your service from anything a client could achieve with home coloring. Design options are endless. However, the following are common ways of determining and planning color placement.

Color Within Zones

Zones or **Zonal Patterns** subdivide the head into multiple areas to create a color design with a combination of colors. Depending on the desired effect, some zones may be left natural. Examples of areas that can be colored in zones are:

- » Fringe
- » Top
- » Crown
- » Nape
- » Perimeter

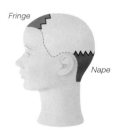

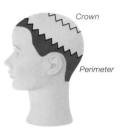

Color Within Shapes

Geometric shapes are often used to describe specifically shaped zones. The size and position of these shapes are determined by your design decisions. Shapes are then further subdivided with partings to achieve varying patterns in the result. Shapes commonly used in color designs are:

- » Rectangles
- » Triangles
- » Circles or portions of circles

DISCOVER**MORE**

Think of your design principle as the arrangement pattern you want to display in the finished result. Is it one rich color with maximum shine all over? Is it a harmonious interplay of fine multicolored strands? Or is it a bold accent in a specific area? Search online for examples of the four design principles used in color design.

DESIGN PRINCIPLES

Design principles are artistic arrangement patterns for the design elements of:

- » Form
- » Texture
- » Color

In color design, it's critical to determine the desired design principle, since this choice determines the patterns, placement and overall end result. In addition, design principles offer you easily understood terms to describe your color results to your clients.

Repetition
Created by applying, or repeating, one color in a given area or throughout or within a zone or shape. A repetition of color creates maximum light reflection and shine.

Alternation
Color alternation means colors change from one to another repeatedly. Two or more colors can be used in an alternation to break up light reflection. Results create the illusion of height and depth or texture. Color alternations can be created throughout the style or within zones and shapes.

Progression
Progression in hair color refers to an ascending or descending scale of colors. These colors can progress from lighter to darker and/or from warmer to cooler. Progressions can be created with zonal patterns or also along the hairstrand.

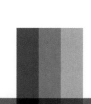  

Contrast
Contrast describes a relationship of opposites. Contrasting colors need to be at least three levels apart from one another. Darker colors create depth, while lighter colors seem to come forward, creating the illusion of volume.

CHANGE THE COLOR, CHANGE THE EFFECT

Color design can have a positive effect on a client's appearance, affecting how she or he looks and feels.

Color can be used to add drama while accentuating the cut. The alternation of colors enhances the texture; it is somewhat bold, but does not overpower the uniqueness of the sculpture.

Color can also be used to create a dramatic color transformation. Careful planning and skillful application can create stunning results.

Color can also subtly reduce the amount of gray and can help a client look and feel younger without being obvious.

Once you are able to visualize color design and determine color placement with the design principles in mind, the possibilities are endless.

LESSONS LEARNED

» **Color design allows the designer to visually transform the perception of a design's form and texture and create a focal point.**

» Repetition of one color throughout draws attention away from texture and puts focus on the form. Texture can be emphasized or de-emphasized based on the color patterns used and the degree of difference in the colors chosen.

» When analyzing hair color:
  ▪ At the basic level, you identify lightness/darkness and/or patterns throughout the hair
  ▪ At the detail level, you identify warmth, coolness and intensity
  ▪ At the abstract level, you identify placement of color and the pattern of shapes used

» Color design decisions leading to the desired color design results include:
  ▪ Emphasizing or de-emphasizing the sculpted form
  ▪ Determining the existing and desired levels
  ▪ Choosing color placement and design principles

110ᶜ.3
IDENTIFYING EXISTING HAIR COLOR

INSPIRE //

Your success in hair coloring is built on your ability to identify the existing color you are working with and to choose the right colors in your formulations so you can achieve hair color results that satisfy your clients' needs.

EXPLORE //

Think of a time that you or a friend had their hair colored in a salon. How did you explain what you wanted? Did you use pictures? Did the colorist lead the discussion with questions and show you colored hair swatches as samples?

ACHIEVE //

Following this lesson on *Identifying Existing Hair Color*, you'll be able to:

>> Describe the difference between eumelanin (brown/black pigment) and pheomelanin (red/yellow pigment)

>> Identify the categories for gray hair mixtures of non-pigmented and pigmented hair

>> Identify the natural hair color levels

>> Explain how manufacturers identify and name artificial hair colors, including by level and tone, and by tone or name

>> Review the hair analysis considerations prior to a color service, including texture and porosity

FOCUS //

IDENTIFYING EXISTING HAIR COLOR

Identifying Natural Hair Color

Identifying Artificial Hair Color

Additional Considerations

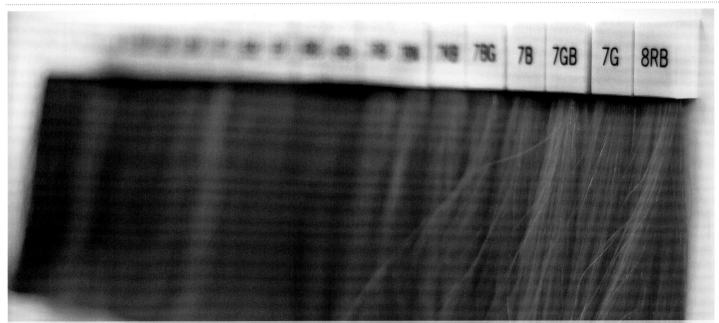

However amazing the idea or vision for a hair color might be, it will only become a reality when the characteristics of the existing hair color are properly identified and compared against the characteristics of the desired hair color. This assessment, in addition to considering the qualities of the hair you're working with, will allow you to choose and formulate the right color(s) to realize your vision. Swatches from manufacturers' color charts can be used as a tool for this assessment.

110°.3 | IDENTIFYING EXISTING HAIR COLOR

After agreeing on the color design decisions, the next critical step is to identify the client's natural or existing hair color. Whenever hair colors are applied, the final result is based on the existing or contributing pigment and the artificial color applied. **Contributing** pigment is either the client's naturally present melanin or a combination of this melanin and any previously applied artificial color that is remaining on the hair.

CONTRIBUTING PIGMENT   +   ARTIFICIAL PIGMENT   =   FINAL COLOR RESULT

IDENTIFYING NATURAL HAIR COLOR

In the following section, you'll learn about how the infinite variety of natural hair colors in the world is created.

MELANIN

Pigment that gives hair its natural color is known as melanin and is determined through genetic coding. This section reviews the information presented in the *Hair Theory* lesson. The three layers of the hair are:

>> Cuticle
>> Cortex
>> Medulla

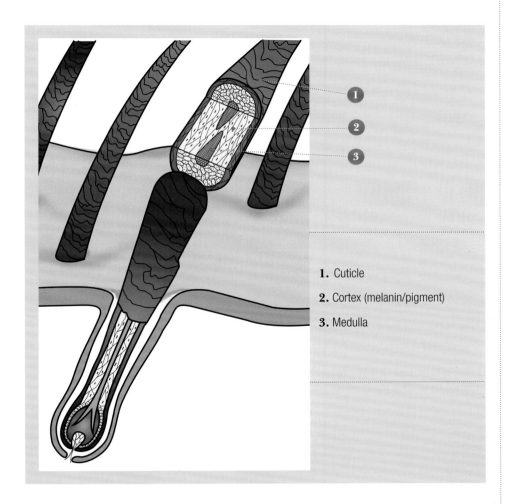

1. Cuticle

2. Cortex (melanin/pigment)

3. Medulla

Down in the hair bulb are pigment-producing cells called melanocytes, which produce small egg-shaped structures called melanosomes. Melanosomes are protein packets that surround pigmented granules called melanin. Melanin eventually becomes incorporated into the keratin protein of the cortex as the hair grows. Melanin develops its color according to its inherent characteristics as the hair grows.

There are two types of melanin found in the cortex of the hair:

>> **Eumelanin (black/brown pigment):** A dense concentration will produce very dark hair; a small concentration will produce light (blond) hair

>> **Pheomelanin (red/yellow pigment):** A dense concentration will produce red hair

The amount, type, size and distribution of melanin determine whether hair will be black, brown, red or blond and all natural shades in between.

Black

Brown

Red

Blond

GRAY HAIR

Gray hair is the result of:

>> Melanocyte cells slowing down the production of melanin in the hairstrand, leading to the gradual and eventually complete loss of color

>> Heredity, which is the primary factor

>> A mixture of non-pigmented (white) hair and pigmented hair on the same head

>> More and more melanocyte cells becoming inactive, resulting in more white hair

Gray hair is found in every field of color, from light gray to medium gray to dark gray.

Individuals have different patterns of graying, such as:

>> Front hairline and sideburns first

>> Top and crown area first

>> Varying percentages from front to back

PERCENTAGES OF GRAY HAIR

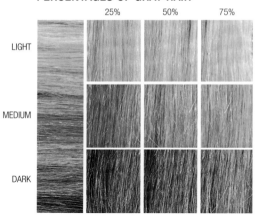

Prior to a color application, it is important to determine your client's percentage of gray since different color formulas accommodate different percentages of gray. Gray hair can be categorized as:

>> 25% gray: More pigmented hair and less non-pigmented hair

>> 50% gray: Even mixture of pigmented and non-pigmented hair

>> 75% gray: Hair will appear lighter overall

■ Adjust this client's formula by applying a color one level darker than the desired level

If the client has approximately 25%-30% gray hair, apply a color one level lighter than the desired shade.

Not every client wants to completely cover his or her gray. Introducing darker-colored strands with customized placement can reduce the appearance of gray hair and add depth.

Other clients will want to completely cover their gray. An all-over, base-to-ends application can be used to deposit color through the entire style. Because of the shorter lengths and exposed hairlines, some male clients will require more frequent retouch appointments.

Gray hair is often more coarse and less elastic, which can make it more resistant to color absorption than pigmented hair. **If you find that you're working with resistant hair, you may need to pre-soften or pre-lighten the hair first by mixing and applying a lighter shade to make it porous enough to receive the final color application.**

IDENTIFYING NATURAL LEVEL AND TONE

Before performing a color service, it's important to:

>> Analyze client's natural hair color

>> Determine its field of color
- Use manufacturer swatches to identify the specific level
- Names and levels may vary with each manufacturer

>> Determine whether the tone is warm or cool

>> Use the color wheel to ask yourself:
- What is the predominant undertone?
- Which side of the color wheel would that fall?

The level of hair color can be identified on a scale of 1-10 or 1-12, with 1 being the darkest and 10 or 12 being the lightest.

DARK	**MEDIUM**	**LIGHT**
1. Black	5. Light Brown	9. Light Blond
2. Dark Brown	6. Dark Blond	10. Very Light Blond
3. Medium Dark Brown	7. Medium Blond	11. Lightest Blond
4. Medium Brown	8. Medium Light Blond	12. Palest Blond

Above you see an example of a 1-12 level scale; know that your color product manufacturer's scale may vary slightly.

SALON**CONNECTION**

Determining Hair Color

Because everyone perceives colors differently, stylists use color swatches to identify the existing hair color.

DISCOVER**MORE**

Show Me the Colors!

Levels of melanin can vary over time, causing a person's hair color to change, and it's possible to have hair follicles of more than one color on the same person. Research the world population percentages to find out which field of color is most prevalent.

IDENTIFYING ARTIFICIAL HAIR COLOR

Being able to identify artificial color is critical from two perspectives in color transformations. For one, when a client has had a prior hair color service, you will need to identify the existing artificial color in addition to the natural level and tone. Secondly, you'll need to identify the desired color outcome based on its level and tone. These steps are necessary for choosing and formulating not only the color shades and products but also the application techniques and the developers that will be used.

Manufacturers identify and name their artificial hair colors in several ways, including:

>> By level and tone, such as 5RV (red-violet)

>> By field and tone, such as medium red-violet

>> By tone or name, such as red-violet or mahogany

TONES/BASE COLORS

In artificial hair coloring, the predominant tone, known as **base color,** identifies the warmth, coolness or neutrality of a color. Understanding base colors helps you to:

>> Understand artificial hair colors

>> Choose the correct level and tone to achieve the desired warm, cool and neutral results

Keeping the color wheel in mind, as well as the client's contributing pigment, will help you choose the right base color to achieve the specific hair color result.

BASE COLOR	RESULT
Yellow or Gold	Golden blond tones
Red	Vibrant red tones; can neutralize green tones
Blue	Minimize orange brassiness
Violet	Neutralize unwanted yellow tones

BASE COLORS

- Ash (A)
- Yellow (Y)
- Blue (B)
- Green (G)
- Gold (G)
- Neutral (N)
- Red-Orange (RO)
- Red (R)
- Red-Violet (RV)
- Violet (V)
- Blue-Violet (BV)

TONES/BASE COLORS

The list on the left will help you become familiar with some of the most common base colors and their abbreviations. The list on the right will help you become more familiar with some of the names for artificial hair colors and their corresponding base colors. These hair colors come in a variety of levels and intensities and can be used alone or mixed together to create a wide array of tones. Keep in mind that artificial hair color names and level numbers may vary slightly with each manufacturer.

ARTIFICIAL HAIR COLORS

- Platinum (Violet)
- Golden Blond (Yellow or Gold)
- Ash Blond (Blue-Violet)
- Chestnut Brown (Green)
- Golden Brown (Gold)
- Copper Gold (Orange)
- Auburn (Red-Orange)
- Burgundy (Red-Violet)
- Mahogany (Red-Violet)
- Plum Brown (Red-Violet)
- Black Velvet (Violet)
- Blue Black (Blue)

Similar to working with natural melanin, when identifying artificial hair color you'll also need to recognize its intensity. The intensity of an artificial hair color can be lessened or neutralized by adding a color that is complementary to its base color into the formula. Or, the color could be intensified by adding a concentrate of a primary or secondary color. These concentrates are often referred to as intensifiers.

The hair swatches shown here are all a level 7. However, they have varying intensities due to different amount red-orange pigment.

BRINGING COLOR DESIGN INTO FOCUS

The perception of color is personal and subjective. Using the fields of color and what you've learned so far about base color/tone and intensity helps you have a successful client consultation.

Remember, the five fields of color are:
>> Dark
>> Medium Dark
>> Medium
>> Medium Light
>> Light

The tones within each field can be referred to as:
>> Warm
>> Cool
>> Neutral

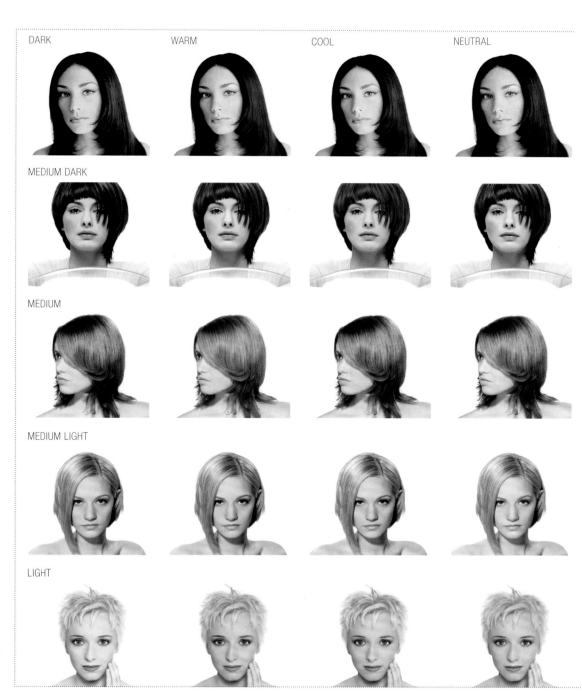

ADDITIONAL CONSIDERATIONS

In addition to level, tone and intensity, it's important to consider the texture (diameter) and porosity of your client's hair. These considerations will influence color absorption and processing time.

TEXTURE

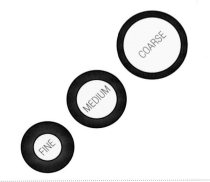

Texture: The degree of coarseness or fineness in the hair fiber

Coarse hair:
>> Resistant to lightening
>> May appear to process slightly lighter than intended level when depositing color

Medium hair:
>> Has an average response to color products

Fine hair:
>> Generally less resistant
>> May appear to process darker when color is deposited
>> When lightening or removing pigment, a mild lightener is recommended

POROSITY

Porosity: The ability of hair to absorb moisture, liquids or chemicals

Porosity is the main factor when selecting products, formulating hair colors and determining the appropriate application technique and amount of processing time.

>> Degree of porosity is determined by number of cuticle layers and how tightly they overlap
>> Raised cuticle layer: Easier for product to penetrate through the cuticle into the cortex

Factors that affect porosity:
>> Sun exposure
>> Alkaline shampoos
>> Chemical products
   - Hair colors
   - Lighteners
   - Perms
   - Relaxers

>> Heat from hair dryers and curling irons

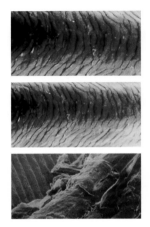

Resistant porosity:
Cuticles are smooth, tightly packed and compact; color absorption may take longer or you may need to apply additional pigment

Average porosity:
Cuticle is slightly raised, accepts color products easily

Extreme porosity:
Cuticle is lifting or missing; hair may take color too intensely or not be able to hold color causing it to fade quickly

Often, clients with long hair may exhibit uneven or varied porosity, because the hair ends have been more exposed to environmental elements.

Causes include:
>> Repeated shampooing
>> Thermal heat
>> Highlights
>> Perms
>> Relaxers

In cases of uneven or extreme porosity, a filler may be required to equalize porosity throughout the hairstrand prior to the color service.

To determine porosity, select a small section of hair. Hold the ends and slide your thumb and forefinger along the strand toward the scalp. The more rough the hair feels and the easier the hair backcombs, the greater the porosity.

Your success in color formulation is built on your ability to develop a trained and experienced eye to identify the level and tone of your client's existing hair color, as well as the desired hair color.

LESSONS LEARNED

>> Eumelanin is brown/black, and pheomelanin is red/yellow

>> Gray hair can be identified as 25%, 50% or 75% gray, and color formulas should be adjusted accordingly

>> Hair color levels range from 1 being the darkest to 10 or 12 being the lightest

>> Texture and porosity influence color absorption and processing time

>> When changing the color of hair, remember to:

■ Determine client's existing level and tone

■ Identify actual hair color
• Natural
• Gray
• Previously color treated
• Use color swatches

■ Consider texture and porosity

110^c.4 | NONOXIDATIVE
COLOR PRODUCTS

EXPLORE //

What are some ways you think you could incorporate nonoxidative color choices into your salon repertoire? Which salon clients do you feel could benefit most from these services?

INSPIRE //

There are many people who like to experiment and push the edge of fashion with their hair color. Hair color products have evolved and allow clients to make a statement without damaging their hair, as in previous years. Nonoxidative colors offer this without any long-term commitment.

ACHIEVE //

Following this lesson on *Nonoxidative Color Products,* you'll be able to:

>> Identify the two main types of nonoxidative color products

>> Describe the characteristics of temporary color products

>> Describe the characteristics of semi-permanent color products

>> Describe the characteristics of vegetable, metallic and compound dyes

FOCUS //

NONOXIDATIVE COLOR PRODUCTS

Temporary Colors

Semi-Permanent Colors

Vegetable, Metallic and Compound Dyes

Nonoxidative color products are beneficial to a broad variety of clients. They are ideal for clients looking to change their existing hair color without the commitment associated with longer-lasting color product choices. Others love nonoxidative color options because they can produce very subtle changes and color enhancements. Then there are those who love using nonoxidative color products to keep their color fresh and vivid between salon visits.

110ᶜ.4 | NONOXIDATIVE COLOR PRODUCTS

Manufacturers create a vast array of nonoxidative color products. Before you begin to use these colors, you need to understand how each one works.

Nonoxidative colors:

» Used to darken, impart shine, add new tones and neutralize unwanted tones

» Add pigment but don't lighten existing hair color

» Are not mixed with a developer or oxidant

» Are used directly out of the bottle or container

» Create a physical change to the hair with no chemical change

» Deposit colors that shampoo out

» Depending on hair porosity can penetrate the cortex, stain the hair and may be difficult to remove

» Major classifications are temporary and semi-permanent colors

TEMPORARY COLORS

*Large Color Molecules
Coat
the Cuticle*

Color Application Final

Color Result

Temporary colors:

>> **Create temporary color changes that last from shampoo to shampoo**

>> Usually applied to clean towel-dried hair

>> **Contain large color molecules that coat only the surface of the hair shaft and cuticle, creating a physical change**

>> **No lightening or chemical changes occur**

>> **Nonreactive, direct dyes, which means no chemical reaction is needed to develop them**

>> Deposit pigment to hair without chemically altering the structure of the hair

>> Also called certified colors

>> Accepted by the government for use in foods, drugs and cosmetics

>> **Do not require a predisposition test since temporary colors do not contain aniline derivative substances**

  ▪ **A predisposition test, also called a patch test, tests for allergic reactions or sensitivity to aniline derivative substances**

DISCOVER**MORE**

Nonoxidative colors have a whole new meaning in today's salon market, far beyond weekly rinses to go along with roller sets. Available as hair chalks, hairsprays, powders, mascaras and more, they range from natural colors for retouching, to bold, vivid colors that make a statement without commitment to constantly upkeep.

Temporary colors, also known as color rinses, are applied to clean, towel-blotted hair. You do not rinse the color out of the hair.

Examples of temporary hair colors include:

Weekly rinses:
- Generally applied at the shampoo bowl
- Used to add tone to faded hair
- Neutralize unwanted tones
- Temporarily add color to hair without creating a chemical change

Color mousses and gels:
- Come in a variety of colors
- Brighten existing color
- Tone gray hair
- Create dramatic effects
- Help in the styling process

Color chalks, crayons and mascaras:
- Come in a variety of colors
- Used for a number of effects ranging from blending new growth to creating fun, colorful designs

Pomades:
- Come in a variety of colors
- Add shine, tone or create special color effects on the hair

Spray-on colors:
- Come in an aerosol can in a variety of colors
- Quick and easy way to add color and create special effects

Color-enhancing shampoos and conditioners:
- Maintain existing color after a color service
- Add tones to hair
- Eliminate unwanted tones

Large Color Molecules Coat the Cuticle

Color Application

Final Color Result

A polymer is a chemical compound or mixture of compounds that consists of many molecules in a long chain-like structure. It's found in many products, including nonoxidative and oxidative hair colors. It can add shine or conditioning qualities to the hair, or it can be used as a thickening agent in a hair coloring product. When applied to the hair, it acts as a coating.

SEMI-PERMANENT COLORS

A wide array of semi-permanent colors, also referred to as glosses or color enhancers, are used to create subtle to dramatic color changes. They can:

>> Add tone or deepen existing color
>> Refresh a faded hair color
>> Neutralize unwanted tones
>> Cover small percentages of gray or blend higher percentages of gray
>> Have a longer-lasting effect when applied with heat to porous hair

Semi-permanent colors:
>> **Deposit color but cannot lighten hair**

>> **Color molecules are overall smaller in size and weight than temporary color molecules**

>> Contain large and small color molecules

 ▪ Smaller color molecules penetrate the cuticle layer and enter the cortex, instead of temporary colors, which coat the hairstrand

>> **Depending on color chosen and hair porosity, color will gradually fade after each shampoo**

>> **Last through several shampoos, then generally wash out**

>> **Leave no line of demarcation**

 ▪ A **line of demarcation** is an obvious difference between two colors along the hairstrand. Can be a result of new growth or overlapping of product onto previously color-treated hair

 ▪ **Since there is no line of demarcation, retouches are not required**

>> **Consist of dye molecules in a solution**

>> **Slightly alkaline in pH**

>> Use a direct dye process that requires no mixing and the color seen in the bottle is the color being deposited onto hair

Although semi-permanent hair colors are not mixed with a developer, check your product's ingredients. A predisposition test for allergic reactions is required if the product contains an aniline derivative ingredient.

Depending on the ingredients in the product and the porosity of the hair, repeated applications of semi-permanent colors may alter the structure of the hair, especially when applied to hair that has been permed or relaxed.

White

Light Field

Medium Light Field

Medium Field

Medium Dark Field

Dark Field

Dark/50% Gray

NONOXIDATIVE

Applying different manufacturers' nonoxidative products on different fields of hair color swatches allows you to analyze the results before working on clients. Remember, these products cannot lighten existing hair color. To better replicate hair that is heated from the scalp, heat the swatches using a blow dryer before applying the products. The resulting color is a combination of the color applied and the existing hair color.

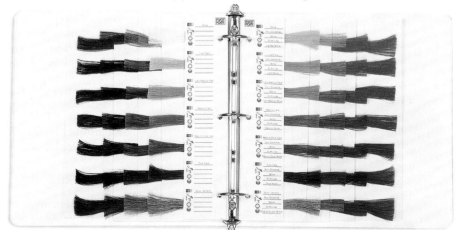

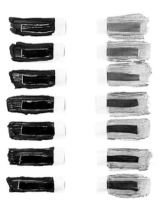

VEGETABLE, METALLIC AND COMPOUND DYES

Vegetable, metallic and compound dyes are the least common types of hair coloring products used in the salon and fall into the nonoxidative color category. Although some areas of the world still use vegetable dyes in the salon, metallic and compound dyes are discouraged since they are unreliable and sometimes unsafe. The metals in a henna compound dye may react violently with other chemicals used in the salon, causing breakage and discoloration. The more these colors are used, the more change takes place, which is why they're also called progressive colors.

VEGETABLE DYES

>> Utilize natural products to color the hair

>> **Henna:**
- **The most common vegetable dye**
- **In its purest form, provides reddish highlights in the hair**
- One of the oldest forms of hair coloring
- Derived from the Egyptian privet plant
- To create colors other than red, it is mixed with metallic salts, such as lead, silver and copper
- Can penetrate the cortex after a few applications and build up, causing the color to become permanent

Henna powder

VEGETABLE DYES (cont'd)

» **Hair that has been colored with henna shouldn't be permed since the build-up doesn't allow the reforming and neutralizing solutions to penetrate evenly**

» Chamomile is found in shampoos and after-shampoo rinses
- Relatively harmless to the hair
- Produces a yellow stain on the hair resembling golden highlights

METALLIC DYES

» **Known as progressive or gradual dyes because the hair turns darker with each application or over time due to air exposure**

» Not considered a professional product

» Metals in the product do not mix successfully with other chemicals used in salon services, such as perm solutions
- Mixing these products can cause discoloration and breakage
- It's advisable to cut the hair to remove the unwanted metallic dye

» May fade into peculiar or unnatural shades when exposed to sun and chlorine; silver dyes may appear to have a green cast; lead dyes a purple cast; copper dyes a red cast

COMPOUND DYES

» **Are a combination of metallic and vegetable dyes**

» Metallic salts are added to vegetable dyes to create a wider range of colors and a longer-lasting color

» Tend to be unpredictable and are incompatible with other chemical services in the salon

TEST FOR METALLIC SALTS

If you suspect metallic salts are present, perform a "1:20 test" prior to performing a chemical service. This test is done by mixing 1 ounce (30 ml) of 20 volume (6%) developer and 20 drops of 28% ammonia in a glass bowl. Remove at least 20 strands of hair and immerse in mixture for 30 minutes. At the end of 30 minutes, look for any of these possible results:

» If the hairstrands lighten slightly, there are no metallic salts present. You may proceed with service.

» If the hair lightens quickly, the hair contains lead. Do not perform a chemical service.

» If there is no reaction after 30 minutes, the hair contains silver. Do not perform a chemical service.

» If the solution begins to boil, gives off an unpleasant odor, and if the hair degrades and pulls apart easily, the hair contains copper. Do not perform a chemical service.

Nonoxidative colors allow many people to experiment and push the edge of fashion with their hair color. Understanding nonoxidative color products allows you to offer subtle to dramatic color changes, while maintaining the integrity of the hair.

SALON**CONNECTION**

Color Adjustments

When working with nonoxidative colors, think of liquid color products like you would a lipstick stain. Sometimes they can look very dark when they come out of the tube, but they are actually fairly transparent. The level of hair that you are applying the nonoxidative color to will determine the brightness—when applied over very light hair, or the richness—when applied over dark hair. When applying over hair that is graying, you get a very dimensional color due to the variance in the natural hair color.

LESSONS LEARNED

>> Nonoxidative colors add pigment through a physical change but do not lighten existing hair color. The major classifications of nonoxidative colors are temporary and semi-permanent.

>> Temporary colors are a direct dye that coats the hair shaft.

>> Semi-permanent hair colors are a direct dye and can enter the cuticle layer and may require a predisposition test.

>> Vegetable, metallic and compound dyes are referred to as progressive or gradual colors and should be identified in the hair before beginning any chemical service, as they may cause adverse reactions. They are incompatible with other chemical services in the salon.

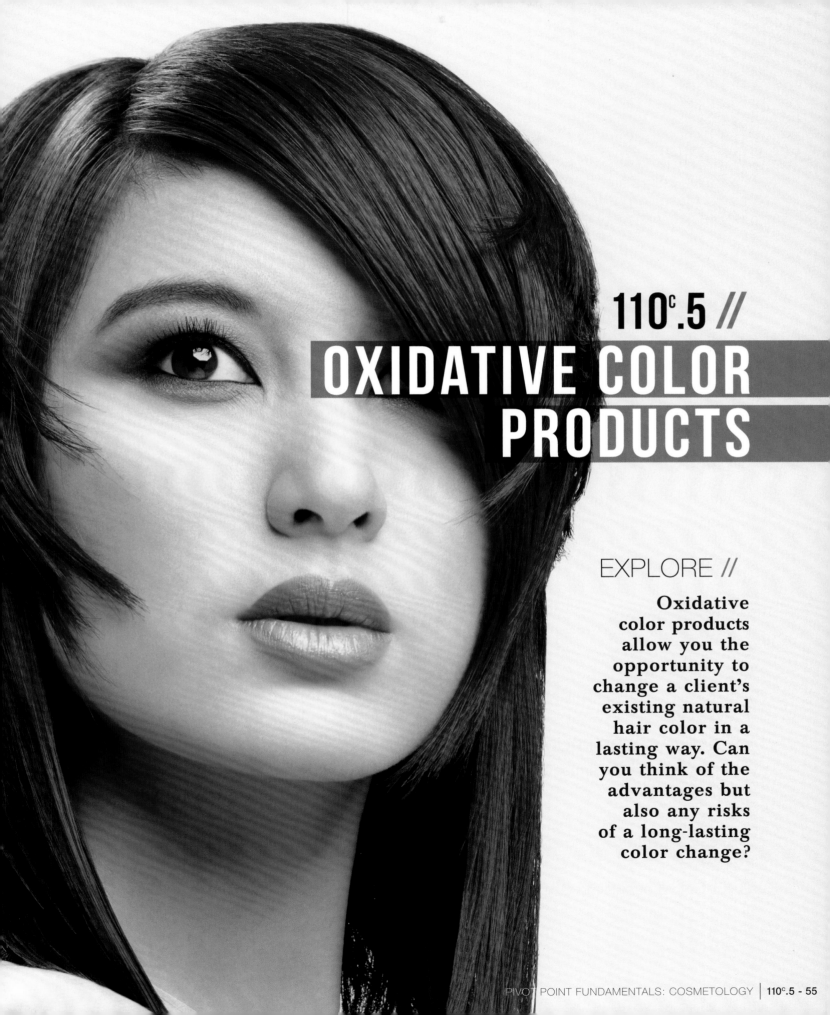

110ᶜ.5 //
OXIDATIVE COLOR PRODUCTS

EXPLORE //

Oxidative color products allow you the opportunity to change a client's existing natural hair color in a lasting way. Can you think of the advantages but also any risks of a long-lasting color change?

INSPIRE //

Oxidative colors are the foundation for color business in the salon. Mastering how they work allows you limitless creative expression with hair color services.

ACHIEVE //

Following this lesson on *Oxidative Color Products*, you'll be able to:

>> Identify the two types of oxidative color products

>> Explain the relationship of developer strength and levels of the desired color

>> Describe the characteristics of fillers, concentrates, intensifiers and drabbers

>> State the difference between on-the-scalp lighteners and off-the-scalp lighteners

>> Identify the 10 stages of decolorization

>> List four main steps in color formulation

FOCUS //

OXIDATIVE COLOR PRODUCTS

Long-Lasting Semi-Permanent (Demi-Permanent) Colors

Permanent Colors

Developers

Fillers, Concentrates, Intensifiers and Drabbers

Lighteners

Basic Color Formulation Guidelines

Oxidative hair colors allow you the opportunity to permanently change a client's hair color. It's a larger commitment from the client's side, but the range of color options available is limitless. Learning how to use oxidative color, sometimes on its own and sometimes in conjunction with nonoxidative color products, allows you the freedom to take your creativity to the next level. Everything you've learned about color up to this point will contribute to the color formulation process.

110ᶜ.5 |
OXIDATIVE COLOR PRODUCTS

Oxidative hair color products have become one of the most popular color products used in the salon, since they offer the colorist a wide range of color possibilities. The stylist or colorist can choose from many levels and tones to create an infinite number of hair color results.

Oxidative colors deposit color, or lift (lighten) and deposit color in a single-process technique.

Oxidative colors:

>> Are mixed with an oxidant (developer) to create a chemical change (release of oxygen)
  - This change has a longer-lasting effect than semi-permanent colors

The major classifications of oxidative colors are:

>> Oxidative colors without ammonia:
  - Known as long-lasting semi-permanent, which is also more commonly referred to as demi-permanent hair color

  - Designed to add tone or darken existing hair color

>> Oxidative colors with ammonia:
  - Known as permanent hair color

  - Designed to:
    • Add tone

    • Darken the existing level to achieve a darker result

    • Lighten and add tone to natural hair to achieve a lighter result in a single process

TONE

DARKEN AND TONE

LIGHTEN AND TONE

Manufacturers label their products with the level system and descriptive words similar to the fields of color. Consider the fields of color to be a general classification and levels a more specific description of the lightness or darkness. Keep in mind, darker oxidative colors contain more pigment, while lighter colors contain less pigment but have greater lifting ability. The illustration below visualizes the concentration of pigment in a hair color line that ranges on a level scale from 1-10. Understanding the reduced pigment concentration in lighter colors is especially important when formulating color for grey hair.

DARK		MEDIUM DARK		MEDIUM		MEDIUM LIGHT		LIGHT	
1	2	3	4	5	6	7	8	9	10

LONG-LASTING SEMI-PERMANENT (DEMI-PERMANENT) COLORS

Long-lasting semi-permanent (demi-permanent) colors:

>> **Use a low volume of hydrogen peroxide to develop the color molecules and aid in color processing**
>> **Can only deposit color, add tone to the hair, but not lift (lighten) the existing natural hair color**
>> Contain small color molecules that penetrate the cortex, some of which join or link together
>> **Generally last 4 to 6 weeks, depending on client's hair porosity**
>> **Contain very little or no ammonia,** which is why these products do not lighten the hair
>> **Referred to as deposit-only demi-permanent, or oxidative without ammonia colors**

Small color molecules enter the cortex, some couple together

Color Application   Final Color Result

Oxidative colors are not designed to lift or lighten artificial pigment. However, color removers and dye solvents can be used to lighten or break down and remove artificial pigments.

Nonoxidative colors and oxidative color formulas with low-volume developers are a good choice for clients who relax their hair.

PERMANENT COLORS

Also referred to as aniline derivative tints, permanent colors penetrate the cuticle and cortex and remain on the hair until they are removed by chemical means, or until the hair grows out and is cut off. Their primary ingredient is usually para-phenylenediamine or a related chemical.

Permanent colors:

>> **Sometimes called oxidative tints with ammonia, or aniline derivative tints**

>> **Mixed with hydrogen peroxide developers**

>> **Capable of both lightening natural pigment and depositing artificial pigment in a single process**

>> **Combination of the ammonia and hydrogen peroxide allows the lifting and lightening of the hair's natural color**

>> The stronger the hydrogen peroxide (developer), the greater the lift achieved

>> **Add tone or darken existing hair color**

>> Can reproduce natural shades without losing shine

>> Can be safely applied over hair that has been previously colored or permed

>> **Contain small colorless molecules (para-dyes) that become colored when mixed with hydrogen peroxide**
  - After initial application, the oxidative color swells the hairstrand

  - Small colorless molecules enter the hair with the aid of an alkaline substance such as ammonia

  - As they oxidize in the cuticle and cortex, they link or couple together to form permanent colored molecules which causes them to permanently anchor in the hair

>> **High-lift tints are permanent colors designed to achieve lighter color and generally use 30 or 40 volume hydrogen peroxide.**

>> **Products such as color removers or dye solvents can be used to remove unwanted artificial pigment.**

>> **Once the unwanted pigment is removed, you may recolor the hair as desired.**

Para-phenylenediamine (para-PHE-ni-line-i-DIA-min) and para-toluenediamine (para-tol-U-ene-i-DIA-min) are two types of dye intermediates, either one of which can be found in permanent tints

Small color molecules enter the cortex, some join together

Color Application   Final Color Result

If you are not able to achieve the desired amount of lift with a single-process color (up to 4 levels lighter) prelightening may be required.

DEVELOPERS

Permanent hair colors come in three forms:

>> Liquid:
- Thinner than creams and gels
- Generally applied with an applicator bottle
- May contain fewer conditioning agents and greater ammonia content
- Good penetration ability

>> Cream:
- Generally mixed with a cream developer
- Applied with a bowl-and-brush technique
- Have conditioners and thickening agents

>> Gel:
- Consistency is somewhere between that of a liquid and a cream
- More penetrating than creams
- Fewer conditioning agents

Permanent hair colors are mixed with various strengths of developer, depending on the desired amount of lift and/or deposit. High-lift tints are designed to achieve lighter colors and are generally mixed with a double amount of 30 volume (9%) or 40 volume (12%) hydrogen peroxide. When mixing permanent hair colors, be sure to follow the manufacturer's directions since the amount or volume of peroxide can affect the lift and deposit achieved.

Developers, with a pH of 2.5 to 4.5, are oxidizing agents used with demi-permanent and permanent colors, lighteners and toners. A developer may be referred to as a catalyst or conductor and needs to be mixed with ammonia or other alkaline compounds to become active. Developers come in a variety of strengths (volumes or percentages) and consistencies (liquids or creams). Lower strength developers are used for depositing, and higher strengths are used for greater lift. Follow the manufacturer's directions in selecting the strength and amount of developer to use with oxidative colors. **Hydrogen peroxide (H_2O_2) is the most commonly used developer (oxidizing agent) in hair color products.**

A hydrometer is used to measure the strength (volume) of hydrogen peroxide. It tells the potency of the hydrogen peroxide and allows dilution of higher strengths to lower volumes. A hydrometer can also help determine if an old bottle of hydrogen peroxide is still potent. Manufacturers indicate **shelf life (usually 3 years) and instruct that it be stored in a cool, dry place.**

DISCOVER**MORE**

Shelf Life

The shelf life of developer is usually 3 years. This is true when the cap is replaced immediately after dispensing it into your formula. Research what happens to developer when you leave the cap off for long periods of time. After researching the affects, do you think it would be safe to continue using the developer in your formulas? Do you think you'll continue to achieve predictable results?

>> Alert! >> Increasing the strength of hydrogen peroxide in a formula beyond the manufacturer's recommendations may cause damage to the hair and chemical burns to the skin and scalp.

In the United States, developers are measured by volume: 10, 20, 30 and 40, while in Europe they are measured by percentages: 3%, 6%, 9% and 12%.

The lower the volume, the less lift will be achieved; the higher the volume, the more lift will be achieved. The greater the lift, the more the natural undertones will become visible in the hair. Depending on how much warmth you want to see in the final result, add a complementary color to your formula to cancel out the warmth and maintain a more neutral tone.

40 VOL = 12%

30 VOL = 9%

20 VOL = 6%

DEVELOPER STRENGTHS:

10 volume/3% peroxide or less:
>> Is used for deposit and minimal lift

>> Used with demi-permanent colors

>> Most demi-permanent manufacturers have their own recommended developer of low strength peroxide

20 volume/6% peroxide:
>> Lifts up to 2 levels

>> Ideal for gray coverage

>> Used with majority of hair coloring products

30 volume/9% peroxide:
>> Lifts up to 3 levels

40 volume/12% peroxide:
>> Lifts up to 4 levels

>> Commonly used with high-lift tints

Mixing hydrogen peroxide in a metal bowl will cause the formula to become weak. The metal's ions will have an adverse reaction with the hydrogen peroxide. Therefore, always mix the formula in a plastic or glass bowl.

If lower volumes of developer are not available, you can dilute 20 volume (6%) developer with zero volume (0%) developer using the following guidelines:

>> **15 volume (4.5%)**   3 part 20 volume developer + 1 part 0 volume developer

>> **10 volume (3%)**   1 part 20 volume developer + 1 part 0 volume developer

>> **5 volume (1.5%)**   1 part 20 volume developer + 3 parts 0 volume developer

Cream developer needs to be diluted with a cream 0 volume (0%) while liquid developer can be diluted with distilled water.

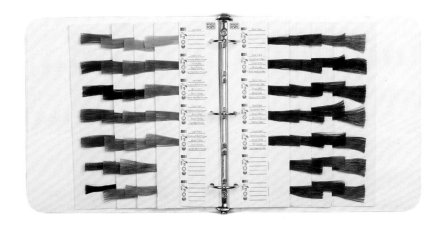

OXIDATIVE COLORS
Applying different manufacturers' oxidative products on different fields of color swatches allow you to analyze the results before working on clients. Remember, these products can add tone, darken the hair or lighten and tone the hair in a single process. The resulting color is a combination of the color applied and the existing hair color.

FILLERS, CONCENTRATES, INTENSIFIERS AND DRABBERS

FILLERS:

- » **Provide an even base color by filling in porous, damaged or abused areas with proteins, polymers or the like**

- » **Equalize the porosity of the hair**

- » **Deposit a base color in one application**

- » Designed to be used prior or in conjunction with the final color formulation

- » **Come in a variety of colors**
  - ▪ **Generally are used to replace the primary color**

- » **Two types:**
  - ▪ **Conditioning:** Used to recondition damaged hair prior to color service; color is applied directly over the filler and processed simultaneously

  - ▪ **Color: Used on damaged hair such as porous hair and when there is a question whether the color will hold**

- » Can be applied directly to the hair before a color or mixed in with the color formula

- » Advantages of fillers:
  - ▪ **Give more uniform color when returning hair to a darker color (tint back)**

  - ▪ Deposit color on faded hair and ends

  - ▪ Help hair hold color

  - ▪ Prevent off-color results

  - ▪ Prevent a dull color appearance

Extremely damaged hair may absorb more color than normal, but it also has a hard time holding on to the color molecules.

CONCENTRATES, INTENSIFIERS AND DRABBERS:

Manufacturers offer a variety of products designed to increase vibrancy of a color or neutralize unwanted tones from contributing pigment:

- » Can be mixed into the color formula or applied directly to prelightened hair to create desired effect

- » Come in a variety of colors:
  - ▪ Yellow, red, blue, orange, violet, green, silver and ash

Concentrates: Used to brighten or neutralize tones

Intensifiers: Used to brighten

Drabbers: Used to neutralize

| *Before* | *Filler Application* | *Color Application* | *Final Color Result* |

LIGHTENERS

In hair lightening, ammonia or other alkalis are used to activate or raise hydrogen peroxide's pH, therefore making it more alkaline. Once activated by the higher pH substance, the peroxide can act as an oxidizer and lift or subtract hair color.

Lightening or bleaching is one of the oldest methods used in a hair color service.

Lighteners, also known as bleach:

» **Utilize ingredients such as ammonia and peroxide to facilitate the oxidation process**
   ▪ Release of oxygen from the peroxide chemically alters other molecules, changes the melanosome (pigment) structure of the hair and lightens the color

» **Used to decolorize, remove or diffuse pigment**

» **Penetrate cortex causing melanin or other pigment to break down before removing or diffusing the color**

» **Always involve oxidation of the natural melanin in the hair**

» Cause the hair to gradually lighten through several color changes as the pigment disperses

» Generally applied to dry hair

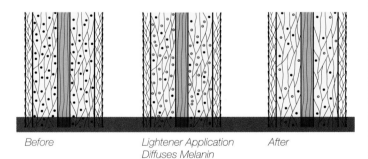

Before   *Lightener Application Diffuses Melanin*   *After*

The longer lightener remains wet and in contact with the hair, the more the melanin and pigments change. Lighteners are classified as either:

» **On-the-scalp:**
   ▪ **Gentle enough to be used directly on the scalp**

   ▪ **Available in two forms:**
      • **Oil lighteners:** Use a certain amount of ammonia to give high lift
         – Mild form of lightener because of the added oil
         – pH is around 9

      • **Cream lighteners: Most popular form of lightener because added conditioners make them gentler and the creamy consistency keeps them in place on the hair, which prevents running or dripping**
         – Used directly on the scalp
         – pH is around 9

   ▪ Activators (accelerator or booster) can be added to oil or cream lighteners to boost strength, which increases the pH and speed of the oxidation process

» **Off-the-scalp (powder bleaches):**
   ▪ **Contain alkaline salts and a strong oxidizing agent that when mixed with peroxide, become a strong lightening product**

   ▪ **Are much stronger than on-the-scalp lighteners and lighten the hair faster**

   ▪ Have no added oils or creams

   ▪ Can irritate the scalp causing burns and blisters

   ▪ Usually used for off-the-scalp lightening procedures such as highlighting

   ▪ Conditioning agents provide some protection to the scalp and hair

   ▪ Some powder lighteners have color pigments already included in their mixture
      • May be used to add desired tones or neutralize certain tones

   ▪ pH is around 10.3

DEGREES OF DECOLORIZATION

As natural hair is lightened, the eumelanin and pheomelanin pigments are decolorized and the hair goes through degrees of decolorization, or stages of lightening. Dark hair goes through approximately 10 stages or degrees of decolorization.

The main degrees to look for are:

>> Red-orange
>> Orange
>> Yellow-orange (gold)
>> Yellow
>> Pale yellow
>> Palest yellow

Hair should never be lightened to white because this could cause extreme damage. If hair is overlightened, a toner may make the hair appear ashy, gray or cool, since most of the warm tones will be missing.

Knowing stages of decolorization and the type of pigments revealed at each level will be critical to your color formulation skills!

| Black | Dark Red-Brown | Red-Brown | Red | Red-Orange | Orange | Yellow-Orange (Gold) | Yellow | Pale Yellow | Palest Yellow |

Time for decolorization always varies with the individual client due to:
>> The amount, size, type and distribution of natural pigment
>> Type and amount of artificial pigment
>> Texture and porosity
>> Difference in products

TONERS

Toners are light pastel colors used to add warmth or coolness to prelightened hair. Toners are used to deposit color and neutralize unwanted tones remaining after prelightening, such as brassy golds or yellows. Refer to the Law of Color and the Color Wheel in the *Color Theory* lesson to help guide the formulation process. Complementary colors will neutralize one another. **For instance, a violet-based toner will produce a light neutral blond on prelightened pale yellow hair.** Perform a strand test in order to predict accurate results. Oxidative toners are mixed with low volumes of developer while nonoxidative toners are not mixed with developer. **Since oxidative toners contain aniline derivatives, a predisposition test is required.** Toners can also be used when there is a mixture of natural and prelightened hair, such as after a highlight service.

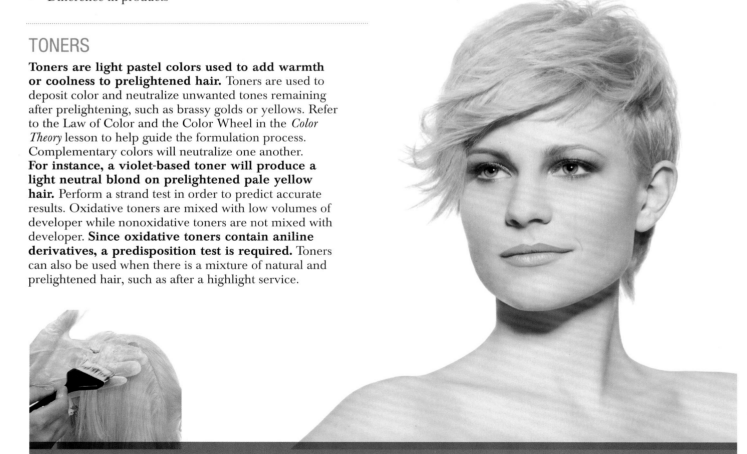

Color Application   *Final Color Result*

Developers work differently with lighteners than they do with color. With color, the developer affects how much lift or deposit your product is able to achieve. For example, if you use a 20 volume (6%) developer with level 9 color on hair that is an existing level 5, your hair will not lift to a level 9. The best you will get is a level 7. With lighteners, however, the developer affects the *speed* the hair will lighten. A 10 volume (3%) developer with lightener will lighten almost as high as a 40 volume (12%) developer will. The difference is, the 10 volume (3%) will take significantly longer. The benefits of lifting slowly are that you have more control over the product and you maintain the integrity of the hair.

DOUBLE-PROCESS

If the desired color result is different than what can be achieved with decolorizing or lightening alone, color can be applied to recolorize the hair to the desired shade. This is referred to as a **double-process technique.** The double-process technique is necessary when you want to lighten your client's hair more than three to four levels lighter since permanent hair color cannot lift more than a maximum of four levels. Before starting the decolorizing (lightening) and recolorizing (adding the pigment back into the hair) process, you need to know the desired color result. This allows you to determine the proper degree of decolorization without over lightening the hair. This will not only maintain the integrity of the hair, it will also allow for more predictable results when toning.

A powder lightener without buffering agents and conditioner can NOT be used for a double process blond procedure.

Before　　　　*Lightener Application Decolorizes*　　　　*Toner Application Recolorizes*　　　　*Final Color Result*

The **double-process technique involves two steps:**

1. **Decolorizing or lightening** the hair to the desired degree. You can lighten selected strands, areas within the design or the entire design.

2. **Recolorizing or toning** the hair by applying an oxidative or nonoxidative color to create the final color result. Generally, a toner is used to recolorize the hair. Since no additional lift can be achieved, use a low-volume developer to achieve the most deposit on the hair.

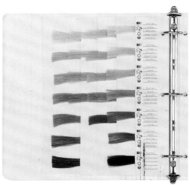

DECOLORIZING

Applying lightener to several swatches of dark hair and watching the hair decolorize will give you a better understanding of the stages or degrees of lightening. Removing the lightener at each degree will help you understand which degrees are most resistant in lightening, while allowing you to analyze the contributing pigment at each degree. The type of lightener you use, the strength of developer and the length of time it remains on the hair will influence your results. Note that the lighter fields of hair color go through fewer degrees of decolorization and will therefore take less time to reach the lighter shades.

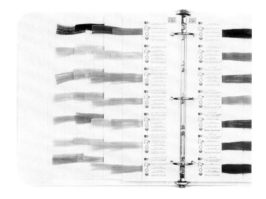

RECOLORIZING

Taking the process one step further by recolorizing the hair will enable you to see the role the contributing pigment plays on the final color result. Remember, it is a combination of the contributing pigment plus the artificial color applied that creates the final color result. Recolorizing the hair with toners to achieve warm, cool and neutral results will give you the opportunity to practice enhancing or neutralizing warm tones. On some swatches vibrant toners were also used to show the intensity that can be achieved on previously lightened hair.

BASIC COLOR FORMULATION GUIDELINES

Now it's time to see how everything you've learned up to this point about color products is put into practice and applied to the formulation process. Formulating requires an understanding of the law of color, the color wheel and underlying pigment that gets revealed when going lighter. No matter what color product line you are working with, this knowledge is the foundation to changing, intensifying or neutralizing your client's existing hair color.

The thought process followed in color formulation can be broken down into four main steps:

Step 1:
Start with a thorough analysis of the level and tone of the existing hair color(s).

Remember to check for:
>> Different colors at the base than the lengths of the hair
>> Different colors in different areas of the head
>> Presence and percentage of any gray hair
>> Whether the existing color is natural, previously colored or a combination of both

Step 2:
Use your hands to feel the texture and porosity of the hair in different areas of the head and along the strand. This will affect how well your color takes without turning out darker or more drab than intended. Also consider your client's individual characteristics like eye color, skin tone and even their personality.

Step 3:
Identify the level and tone of the desired color(s).

Remember to clearly identify:
>> Desired intensity of the tone

>> How many levels darker or lighter you want to go so you will choose the proper developer strength

>> Whether warmth from lightening and breaking down the natural underlying pigment will need to be neutralized for more neutral or cool results

Step 4:
Choose your color product(s) and shade(s) as well as your developer(s) while keeping in mind:
>> In most cases your desired level matches your color product level.

>> Your color product shade will generally match your desired shade, unless you have to compensate for warmth, created from going lighter; in that case you'll need to neutralize with a cooler shade. Or if the result is darker you'll need to add in any missing undertones to the formula so that the final color doesn't look ashy or drab.

>> When staying at the same level or going darker, choose a low developer strength.

>> When going lighter, choose a stronger version.

>> **Always follow manufacturers' guidelines for mixing ratios and processing time.**

After application, set a timer and remember to check periodically to make sure the color is processing correctly and evenly.

Managing Underlying Pigment

The chart below shows with a quick glance the hair color level and their contributing underlying pigments, as well as the color pigments needed to neutralize them.

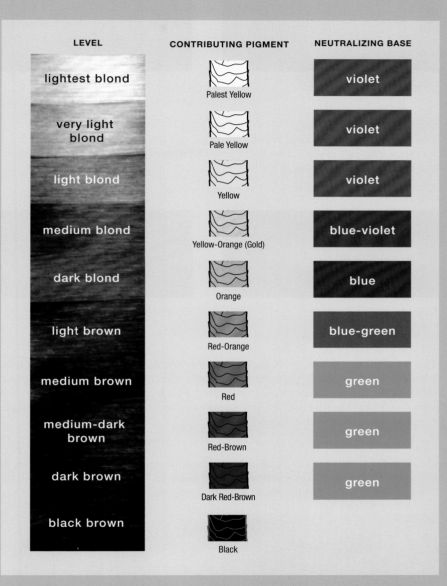

LEVEL	CONTRIBUTING PIGMENT	NEUTRALIZING BASE
lightest blond	Palest Yellow	violet
very light blond	Pale Yellow	violet
light blond	Yellow	violet
medium blond	Yellow-Orange (Gold)	blue-violet
dark blond	Orange	blue
light brown	Red-Orange	blue-green
medium brown	Red	green
medium-dark brown	Red-Brown	green
dark brown	Dark Red-Brown	green
black brown	Black	

SALON**CONNECTION**

Imagine you want to color a client's natural dark brown hair to become medium brown, with a neutral—not reddish—result. You will need to go two levels lighter. At that point, the underlying red pigment will be revealed. Subsequently, your formula needs to include a green pigment to counteract the red and achieve a neutral result.

BASIC COLOR FORMULATION GUIDELINES (CONT'D)

Let's analyze the color formulation examples below:

Color Formula:
Level 6, red-violet

Developer:
20 volume (6%) developer

Existing Level and Tone:
Level 5, golden

Desired Level and Tone:
Level 6, cool red-violet

Why:
The desired color has a cool red shade. Since one level of lift is needed and the desired level is a level 6, the contributing pigment is orange but, only a small amount of orange pigment gets revealed. The formula can be just a little cooler than the target color and mixed with 20 volume (6%) developer.

Color Formula:
Level 8 violet or blue-violet

Developer:
30 volume (9%) developer

Existing Level and Tone:
Level 6, golden

Desired Level and Tone:
Level 8, neutral

Why:
The desired color is two levels lighter than the existing color. To achieve the needed two levels of lift, a 30 volume (9%) developer is used. The contributing pigment at the target color of a level 8 is yellow. Since the desired color is neutral, the warmth of this contributing pigment needs to be neutralized with a complementary pigment, which is violet. Many manufacturers might refer to such a color as ash, silver or cendré. Be sure to learn the actual neutralizing pigments (green, blue or violet) included in the colors you use; color charts very often tell you.

Going further, see how colors were formulated for more complex scenarios on the following examples. As you learned in the lesson on *Color Design,* for multidimensional color results color placement and pattern play a big role and multiple desired shades need to be formulated and combined in the same look.

Existing Level and Tone:
Base: Natural level 4, ends faded level 7
Texture: porous

Desired Level and Tone: Natural level 4
Color Formula: Level 4, natural gold
Developer: 10 volume (3%) developer

Why:
The desired color stays on the same level as the existing color while depositing most of the color onto the ends to achieve a richer result. The desired color is a natural brown shade. Since the color is depositing to a natural tone onto a porous texture, a gold is used in the formula to add back any missing undertones from the faded ends. This will prevent the ends from looking muddy or drab. A 10 volume (3%) developer is used to achieve deposit and shine.

Desired Level and Tone:
Level 7 copper-gold around the face,
level 5-6 warm red through remaining

Color Formula:
Level 8, copper-gold, around face,
½ level 6, red, ½ level 6, red-copper,
through remaining lengths

Developer:
10 volume (3%) developer around face,
20 volume (6%) developer through
remaining lengths

Existing Level and Tone:
Hairline has previously been lightened
to a level 8, gold

Remaining hair is a natural level 4

Why:
The desired color around the hairline is slightly darker than the existing color with a tonal change. Depositing on hair that has been prelightened can cause the hair to pull darker because the lightener causes this hair to become more porous. A level was chosen one level lighter than the intended target color mixed with a 10 volume (3%) developer so the formula could stay on the hair the full intended time to allow for the copper-gold tones to fully penetrate without pulling too dark. The remaining lengths needed to lift 1-2 levels. A level 6, red, was mixed with a level 6, red-copper. Since the natural hair color is lifting, the warm undertones will become more visible adding to the warm red tones. A 20 volume (6%) developer was used to achieve an equal amount of lift and deposit.

Oxidative colors are the foundation for color business in the salon. Mastering how they work allows you limitless creative expression with hair color services. Understanding how to work with oxidative colors will expand your creative skills and help your clients commit to a new look they will love.

LESSONS LEARNED

>> Two main categories of oxidative colors are demi-permanent (long-lasting semi-permanent) and permanent colors.

>> Lower strength developers are used for depositing color and higher strength developers are used for lifting color.

>> Fillers, concentrates, intensifiers and drabbers can be used to modify the intensity, tonality or lasting ability of hair colors.

>> Lighteners applied directly to the scalp are generally mild with a cream or oil consistency. Off-the-scalp lighteners are powder bleaches that contain alkaline salts and are stronger and faster when lifting color from the hair.

>> Hair goes through up to 10 stages of decolorization during which the underlying contributing pigment gets revealed:
- Black
- Dark red-brown
- Red-brown
- Red
- Red-orange
- Orange
- Yellow-orange
- Yellow
- Pale yellow
- Palest yellow

>> The main steps in color formulation include:
- Analyzing the existing hair color's level and tone
- Identifying hair texture and porosity along the strand and in the various areas of the head
- Identifying the desired color's level and tone
- Choosing color products, shades and developer strengths

COLOR TOOLS AND ESSENTIALS | 110^c.6

110ᶜ.6 | COLOR TOOLS AND ESSENTIALS

INSPIRE //

From bold colors to a soft, lived-in look—the choice of tools and products is up to you.

ACHIEVE //

Following this lesson on *Color Tools and Essentials,* you'll be able to:

>> Describe the functions of the main coloring tools

>> Provide examples of supplies, products and equipment used to perform a color service

FOCUS //

COLOR TOOLS AND ESSENTIALS

Color Tools

Color Essentials

o perform professional color procedures, you need a selection of products, tools, supplies and equipment.

COLOR TOOLS

Color tools are the hand-held tools you use. Because different tools have different effects, the tools you choose will impact the final result. Each tool should be selected based on the desired end result and your personal preference as a colorist. Being familiar with each tool will enable you to make the proper selections for the desired results.

COLOR BOWL

The color bowl is used to hold the color formula. Generally, a bowl and brush are used when working with products that have a thick or creamy consistency.

Bowls can have:
» An edge that allows you to rest the color brush

» A rubber base that prevents the bowl from slipping

» A measurement guide that is used for accuracy when mixing

COLOR APPLICATOR BOTTLE

The color applicator bottle is used to apply color that is thinner in consistency.

» Generally has a pointed applicator tip used to part the hair and apply the color

» May have brush-like bristles at the tip or plastic teeth similar to a comb, to comb the product through the hair

» Bottle is marked with numbers that are used as a measuring guide

COLOR BRUSHES

Color brushes consist of nylon bristles on one end that are used to apply color, while the other end is pointed and can be used to part the hair.

» Come in a variety of shapes and sizes

» Chosen according to the size and shape of the area you're working in and the desired effects

COLOR COMBS

A variety of combs for color can be used, each for a different purpose.

Tail Comb

A tail comb is used for combing and parting the hair. They can come with fine teeth or wide teeth, depending on your preference.

» Teeth are used for combing the hair

» Pointed end is used for parting the hair and applying/closing foils

» Metal-tip tail combs are popular because they allow for more precise partings and weaves

Palette Comb

A palette comb is used for a faster, more blended alternative to foiled highlights and in conjunction with painting techniques.

» Teeth at wide end are positioned at base to hold hair close to the scalp and separate the selected strands from surrounding hair during application

» Flat panel surface holds the remainder of the hair while applying

» Used to create more natural and blended results quickly and easily

FOIL

Foils are used to isolate the colored hair from uncolored hair.

» Make sure foils are wider and longer than the section you are coloring

» Commonly used when highlighting

» Also used to isolate sections applied with different colors

THERMAL STRIPS

Thermal strips are also used to isolate the colored hair from uncolored hair.

» Offer better heat transfer throughout the section, promoting faster, more even processing

SALON**CONNECTION**

Foils of a Different Color

If you see different color foils on a client's head during a highlight or lowlight service, it often signals that multiple color products, or formulas, are positioned within the color design.

Colorists identify where they've placed different products by choosing a different color of foil for each formula. This allows them to quickly see the placement pattern as it develops and reminds them which color formula to apply next.

COLOR TOOLS

The following chart summarizes the tools and their related functions.

TOOLS	FUNCTION
Glass or Plastic Color Bowl	Holds color formula; may have an edge to rest color brush and rubber base that prevents slipping; may have a measurement guide used for accuracy in mixing; generally, a bowl-and-brush application is used when working with products of thick consistency
Color Brush	Consists of nylon bristles on one end used to apply color; other end is pointed and used to part hair; brushes come in a variety of shapes and sizes; chosen according to area being worked on and size of sections and parting, as well as desired effects
Color Applicator Bottle	Holds color formula; pointed tip is used to part hair and apply (distribute) color; marked with numbers used for measuring; generally, a bottle application is used when working with products of thinner consistency
Foil/Thermal Strips	Isolate woven or sliced strands of hair from untreated hair during color service; prevent colors from intermixing
Tail Comb	Used for combing and parting hair; fine teeth on one end are used for combing hair and pointed end is used for parting hair
Wide-Tooth Comb	Used for combing in color for special effects and to detangle the hair
Palette Comb	Used in conjunction with painting techniques; more blended alternative to foiled highlights
Clip	Controls hair while coloring

COLOR ESSENTIALS

The following charts will help you become familiar with the various supplies, products and equipment you'll use in the salon.

» Color supplies include single-use items, such as neck strips and gloves and multi-use items, like towels and capes.

» Color products are produced by many different manufacturers, are disposable and must be frequently replaced. Refer to the lessons on nonoxidative and oxidative color products for more information.

» Color equipment includes the furnishings and provisions necessary to provide a professional color service, such as a shampoo bowl.

Keep in mind, employers are required to make Safety Data Sheets (SDS) for all products available for your reference and use in the salon.

COLOR SUPPLIES

SUPPLIES	FUNCTION
Measuring Device	Indicates units of measurement in ounces (oz), milliliters (ml) or cubic centimeters (cc); used to measure color formula
Protective Cape	Protects client and client's clothing
Neck Strip	Protects skin from direct contact with cape
Towels	Used as part of draping procedure to protect client's clothing; used for shampoo service
Cotton Roll	Protects client's eyes from product drips when positioned around hairline; used at base in between partings to avoid product seepage during lightener applications; used to perform patch tests
Protective Apron/Smock for Colorist	Protects colorist's clothing from stains
Protective Gloves	Protect hands during chemical services; in some areas, wearing gloves during any service, especially chemical services, is mandatory—check with your area's regulatory agency
Chemical Service Record	Documents client's personal and color information

COLOR PRODUCTS

PRODUCTS	FUNCTION
NONOXIDATIVE COLOR	
Temporary	Adds tonal value or highlights to specific areas; color washes out when hair is shampooed
Semi-Permanent	Adds tonal value and imparts shine but doesn't lighten natural melanin; gradually fades, lasts 4-6 shampoos; longer-lasting effect on porous hair or when heat is applied; can have a permanent effect on chemically relaxed and lightened hair
OXIDATIVE COLOR	
Demi-Permanent (Long-Lasting Semi-Permanent)	Adds tone or darkens existing color but doesn't lighten natural melanin or previously colored hair; retouches may be required every 4-6 weeks
Permanent	Tones, darkens or lightens natural melanin in a single process; cannot lighten previously colored hair; remains on hair until it's cut off or removed by chemical means, such as with a lightener or color remover; retouches may be required every 3-6 weeks
LIGHTENERS	
On-the-Scalp Lightener	Lightens (decolorizes) natural or artificial pigment; gentle enough to be used on scalp
Off-the-Scalp Lightener	Lightens (decolorizes) natural or artificial pigment; used for off-the-scalp techniques
ADDITIONAL COLOR PRODUCTS	
Hydrogen Peroxide (Developer)	Available in different strengths; used as oxidizing agent for oxidative colors and lighteners
Filler	A color or conditioner that evens out porosity of hair or creates an even base color for final color service
Barrier Cream	Protects skin around hairline from hair color stains
Porosity Equalizer	Evens hair porosity to create an even base color for final color service
Stain Remover	Removes color stains from skin

COLOR EQUIPMENT

EQUIPMENT	FUNCTION
Rollable Color/ Product Table	Provides a place for laying out color tools, supplies and products
Hydraulic Chair	Provides proper back support to client during color service; adjustable
Timer	Allows colorist to keep track of processing time
Disinfectant Container	Holds solution for disinfecting tools
Hood Dryer/Heated Lamps/Accelerator Machines	Used to speed up processing time
Shampoo Bowl/Area	Supports client's neck and holds water and shampoo products during a shampoo service

Understanding the different color tool choices available allows you to make your selection based on the desired end result and your personal preference.

LESSONS LEARNED

>> The six main color tools and their functions include:

- Color Bowl – Used to hold the color formula

- Applicator Bottle – Used to apply color that is thinner in consistency

- Color Brushes – Used to apply color; pointed end can be used to part the hair

- Color Combs:
  - Tail Comb – Used for combing and parting hair
  - Palette Comb – Used for a faster, more blended alternative to foiled highlights

- Foil – Isolates colored hair from uncolored hair

- Thermal Strips – Offer better heat transfer throughout section, promoting faster, more even processing

>> In addition to the color tools, color essentials include the supplies, products and equipment that are needed to perform a color service.

- Supplies include the measuring device, cape and towels

- Color products include the different forms of hair color options, lightener, developer and products to protect against stains

- Equipment includes permanent fixtures, such as the hydraulic chair, timer and shampoo bowl

110ᶜ.7 // COLOR SKILLS

EXPLORE //

Think of the last time you had to learn something new. Was it easy for you at first? Did your skills improve with practice?

INSPIRE //

Mastering the procedural
hair color steps will take you
closer to having confidence in
performing successful color
services in the salon.

FOCUS //

COLOR SKILLS

Color Design Procedures

Color Considerations

ACHIEVE //

Following this lesson on
Color Skills, you'll be able to:

>> State the color procedures in
the sequential order used to
perform a color service

>> Describe each of the six
color procedures

>> Explain additional factors to
consider when coloring hair

110ᶜ.7 | COLOR SKILLS

When designing and performing color services, you need to develop your ability to visualize color placement and color patterns, while taking the hair sculpture into consideration. In *Color Skills*, you'll now focus on the procedural steps performed during the majority of sought-after color design services.

COLOR DESIGN PROCEDURES

The color procedures are a system for producing predictable color results. Developing your technical skills and following a system allows you to achieve efficiency and consistency in your color work.

Designers follow these six color steps as the foundation of their color designs:

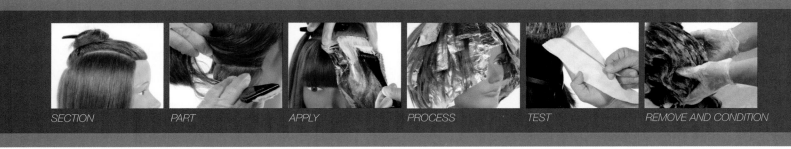

SECTION   PART   APPLY   PROCESS   TEST   REMOVE AND CONDITION

SECTION

Sectioning is used to help map out the placement of color and positioning of foils. It also isolates the area of the design that is going to be accentuated. To achieve the most desirable effects, a thorough analysis of the hair sculpture is needed to see where the lengths will fall when the hair is styled.

RECTANGULAR
>> Positioned to correlate to a center or side part

>> May extend through crown

CIRCULAR
>> Distinguishes color patterns between exterior and interior

TRIANGULAR
>> Isolates sections of hair in fringe

>> Adds interest in a specific focal area

PART

In color design, parting allows you to determine how evident the color pattern is in the final result. The direction and thickness of the parting can determine how bold or subtle the color will appear.

Keep the following in mind:

>> Horizontal slices placed in the interior will create a definite alternation of color.
>> Diagonal slices will create a more blended effect.
>> Partings can be taken in straight lines, resulting in slices.
>> Partings can be woven, as is commonly done for highlights.

The thickness of the parting is determined by considering:

>> Color product consistency
>> Hair density to ensure proper penetration of color
>> Desired boldness or subtleness of end result

Parting Directions

Any lines from the celestial axis can be used to identify parting directions:

>> Horizontal
>> Vertical
>> Diagonal
>> Pivotal
>> Concave
>> Convex

HORIZONTAL

VERTICAL

 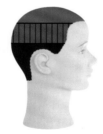

DIAGONAL

PIVOTAL

Zigzag partings can also be used to allow greater transition between zones. The steeper the zigzag parting, the more blended the final result will appear.

Dimensional Coloring Techniques

Dimensional coloring involves the positioning of highlights and/or lowlights to selected strands throughout the design to create special effects.

>> **Highlighting** involves making the isolated strands lighter.

>> **Lowlighting** involves making the isolated strands darker.

Visually, darker colors recede and add depth, while lighter colors come forward and add brightness to the design. Note how in the image to the right the same hair color can appear lighter (highlight) or darker (lowlight), depending on its surrounding color.

After determining the sectioning pattern to position dimensional color, select the appropriate technique(s) to achieve the desired results. Widely used dimensional color techniques include weaving, slicing and freeform painting.

Weaving and Slicing

>> Used to add depth and dimension

>> Used with existing hair color or in conjunction with all-over color application on the remaining hair

>> Lightener and/or color are used to create highlighted or lowlighted effects

>> Amount and thickness of weaves and/or slices determine how bold or subtle final result will be

SALON**CONNECTION**

Pictures Painted With Words

Consultation and communication skills are especially important when clients bring in pictures of how they want their hair color to look. It's your responsibility to explain how these colors may look different based on the surrounding colors in a multi-dimensional service, differences in skin tones, undertones, and how they all play a role in what the final hair color result will look like on them. Clarifying realistic expectations will result in a much more pleasant experience for the client.

WEAVING

The **weaving technique** uses a tail comb to weave out selected strands in an alternating pattern. These strands are then positioned over foil or thermal strips and lightener or color is applied. The woven strands are generally enclosed in the foil or thermal strip to isolate them from the remaining hair.

The size of the weave refers to the amount of hair selected, while the density pattern refers to the amount of weaves within a particular area or parting. The depth of the weave also influences the amount of hair selected.

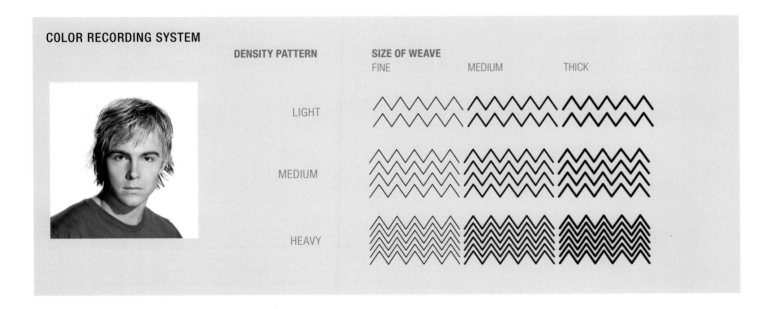

COLOR RECORDING SYSTEM

DENSITY PATTERN

SIZE OF WEAVE

FINE   MEDIUM   THICK

LIGHT

MEDIUM

HEAVY

FINE

MEDIUM

THICK

On curly hair, a medium or thicker weaving technique ensures more visibility of a highlighted or lowlighted area. Too fine of a weave may diffuse too much in curly texture and not give dimension. However, too thick of a weave can become too bold and sometimes looks amateurish.

SLICING

The **slicing technique** uses a tail comb to part off a straight line through the hair. As with weaving, these strands are then positioned over foil or thermal strips, and lightener or color is applied. The slices are also enclosed in foil or thermal strips to isolate them from the remaining hair.

The size of the slice refers to the amount of hair selected, while the density pattern refers to the number of slices within a particular area.

>> Fine slices = Blended appearance

>> Thick slices = Bold appearance

COLOR RECORDING SYSTEM

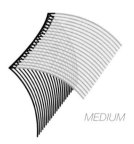

DENSITY PATTERN	SIZE OF SLICE		
	FINE	MEDIUM	THICK
LIGHT			
MEDIUM			
HEAVY			

FINE   MEDIUM   THICK

Slices can also be positioned one on top of another, referred to as a back-to-back technique.

When selecting foils, you want to make sure the foils are wider and longer than the section you're weaving and slicing. If the sections are wider than the foil:

>> The color product may seep out, resulting in "bleeding" or "spotting" on the untreated hair

>> The base area of hair that extends over the side of the foil may not get colored because hair converges to fit the foil

>> Subdivide partings that are too wide to correct these common mistakes

Slices can also be used in a specific area to:

>> Make a fashion statement

>> Create a focal point

FREEFORM PAINTING

Freeform painting is a technique in which a tool or color brush is used to strategically position color or lightener on parts of the hair. This can create a bold or subtle, highlighted or lowlighted effect, depending on the colors chosen. An advantage of the freeform painting technique is a less visible, more natural line of demarcation.

Freeform painting technique:

>> Applied with a brush

>> Painted on the hair

>> Referred to as surface painting

>> Color deposited only on selected strands

>> Can be used for gray reduction technique or quick blended highlights

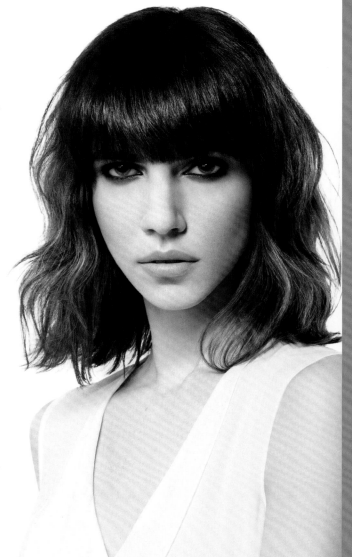

END LIGHTS

End lights are a dimensional color technique that lightens only the ends of the hair. Product can be applied:

>> With a brush

>> To foil and buffed across surface of hair

CAP METHOD

The **cap method** uses a crochet hook to pull hair through a perforated cap. The amount and density of the strands pulled through the cap will determine whether a bold or subtle effect is achieved.

After the strands are pulled through the holes in the perforated cap:

>> Lightener or color is applied

>> A plastic bag is positioned over the color to facilitate processing and keep the product moist

If a toner is required, the application can be performed with the cap in place if using a permanent color, or to keep the untreated hair the original color. Toner can be applied after the cap has been removed if using a semi-permanent color, or to color the untreated hair, which will result in a dimensional tonal change. The cap method should not be performed on hair shorter than 4" (10 cm), since this can result in a spotted look.

SALONCONNECTION

When removing the cap, do so with care. If you remove the cap before you tone the hair, the hair may be tangled. Comb through the lengths before removing the cap to allow the hair to slide back through the holes. This prevents hair from getting stuck and pulling on the hair when it's in a fragile state. If you do not need to tone the hair, apply conditioner, comb the strands and slide the cap off while the conditioner is still in the hair.

RETOUCH FOR DIMENSIONAL COLORING TECHNIQUES

Dimensional coloring techniques usually require a retouch application anywhere from 3 to 12 weeks after the original service.

Retouches consist of:

>> Introducing new highlights or lowlights into the outgrown area of the previously lightened strands

>> Applying product only to the new growth area; overlapping with the existing color can result in breakage or dark bands of color within the strand

Tips for retouch application, when foiling:

>> With long hair, use the tip of your tail comb to sweep the uncolored ends off the foil before folding

>> With short hair, partially fold the foil to cover the untreated hair, then fold the foil the remainder of the way to cover the product

APPLY

Make sure the application is neat and organized to make the client feel more comfortable and prevent staining on the scalp and skin around the hairline.

COLOR APPLICATION TECHNIQUES

Applying color to the hair is typically done with either a bowl-and-brush technique or with an applicator bottle.

Bowl and Brush

>> Popular way to apply cream colors and lighteners

>> Thicker consistency of product allows for clean and accurate placement of color

>> Common method for retouch application

Applicator Bottle

>> Commonly used to apply toners and colors with a thinner consistency, such as most demi-permanent hair colors

>> Application time is generally quicker than using a bowl and brush

COLOR ALONG THE STRAND

As discussed in *Color Design*, knowing where to apply color along the strand plays a big role in achieving desired results.

BASE TO ENDS

Ensure the product thoroughly penetrates the entire strand. Areas that absorb less color will look uneven and have a spotted result.

AWAY FROM THE BASE

Coloring away from the base creates a grown-out or lived-in effect. This technique is popular with clients who request ombré services. Holding the brush vertically or at an angle, while applying will result in an even softer color transition.

BASE

Applying color to the base of the hair is generally referred to as a retouch application.

ENDS

Often performed to achieve a sun-kissed look. Applying color to only the ends of the hair will visually enhance the appearance of texture and movement.

COMBINATION

With color trends continually evolving, colorists will often decide on color placement using a combination of techniques to create a unique personalized design.

After application, the products need time to process. Color products should be timed according to manufacturer's directions, while considering hair porosity. Porous hair absorbs products quickly, which can result in hair processing too dark.

For example: When performing a toner application after using lightener, carefully monitor the color development on the hair.

When working with resistant porosity, such as gray hair, you may apply heat to open the cuticle and allow for better penetration.

DISCOVER**MORE**

Where to Begin?

Colorists need to choose where to begin their application. When creating a darker result, colorists often begin in the area that naturally would be the darkest—in the back. If a lighter result is desired, they often begin where the hair would naturally be the lightest—around the face. In other instances, colorists may choose to begin the application in the area where the greatest color change is needed, or where the hair is more resistant, to allow for longer processing time.

SALON**CONNECTION**

Check along the hairline, ears and neck for any excess color or staining of the skin. Make this your priority immediately after you have completed your application.

TEST

A strand test will allow you to see if the color has developed successfully or if additional processing time is needed. Multiple areas may need to be tested multiple times during color processing. Foils may need to be checked in the area that you first placed them before you have finished applying all of them to ensure the first few foils don't overprocess.

To test the color within a foil:

>> Choose a foil and clip surrounding foils up and away

>> Open foil gently and use tail comb to lift a piece of hair off the foil

>> Position the hair on a paper towel and spray with water

>> Gently rub the color off of the strand to see the development

>> If the color has not fully processed, return to the foil and reapply color

All-over color should be checked where you first applied and also in more resistant areas where processing could take longer.

To strand test an all-over color:

>> Select a small section of hair

>> Position hair on a paper towel and spray with water

>> Gently rub color off strand to see development

>> If color has not fully processed, reapply color

REMOVE AND CONDITION

Once you have reached the desired color and processing is complete, remove the color products thoroughly from the scalp and hair. In most cases, this will be by rinsing and shampooing prior to conditioning. You'll also need to discuss different home care products your client can use to prevent color fading and maintain salon quality results between appointments.

COLOR CONSIDERATIONS

There are many important considerations that can enhance final color results. One special consideration should be the client's sculpture to determine how the color placement will best complement it for the client. Color considerations in this section focus specifically on:

>> Solid form
>> Graduated form
>> Increase-layered form
>> Uniformly layered form

SOLID FORM

The solid form sculpture has lengths that fall to one level at the perimeter, displaying a smooth, unactivated texture. Your choice of color placement and pattern allows you to emphasize the smooth characteristics or de-emphasize them, creating the illusion of surface activation.

Repetition
>> Creates the look of a smooth, shiny surface

>> Enhances angular shape

>> Reflects light more evenly

>> Enhances rich appearance of textured hair

>> Beneficial for clients with dry hair and curly hair

Alternation
>> Draws attention away from form line and visually softens shape

>> Creates illusion of additional texture

>> Lighter colors come forward, while darker colors recede

Contrast
>> Darker colors that peek through bottom draw more attention to blunt perimeter

>> Ideal for clients with fine hair since this emphasizes concentration of weight in perimeter

---

GRADUATED FORM

Most clients who wear the graduated form love the shape, and colorists usually strive to enhance it. Positioning a darker color below the ridgeline will create more depth and the appearance of a closer-fitting nape. Adding lighter colors above the ridgeline will add the illusion of volume and expansion in the interior.

Repetition
>> Enhances silhouette of shape
>> Reflects light more evenly

Alternation
>> Softens form through interior
>> Draws attention to face
>> Showcases closeness in nape

Contrast
>> Creates a focal point
>> Emphasizes angular shape

INCREASE-LAYERED FORM

Many clients benefit from increase layers because they want long hair with the added benefit of shorter lengths for volume and texture. Your choice of color placement and coloring techniques can enhance the activated texture or make the form line appear fuller.

Contrast

>> Contrasting color along the shorter strands and fringe accentuates where activated texture falls and draws attention to face

Progression

>> A progression from darker to lighter visually adds volume to top and fullness to form line

Alternation

>> Creates added textural interest and movement

UNIFORMLY LAYERED FORM

Since the uniformly layered form has consistent lengths throughout, it often resembles a circle. Color considerations include deciding whether you wish to enhance the round shape or visually change the form. Additionally, shorter uniform layers display a lot of texture, and designers should carefully consider whether color should add more texture and how much texture is enough.

Repetition

>> Draws attention to and enhances shape of form

>> Can calm activated texture

Contrast

>> Coloring exterior darker will make form look narrower and closer in shape similar to graduated form

Alternation

>> Creates illusion of additional activation

DISCOVERMORE

Find imagery for each of the four forms, and identify the color placement within each image. Share your results.

The more experience you gain, the more efficient you'll get and the more comfortable you'll feel when creating color designs for clients.

LESSONS LEARNED

» The color procedures include:

1. **Section** – Dividing the hair into workable areas for control

2. **Part** – Subdividing sections and subsections and determining how evident the color pattern is in the final result

3. **Apply** – Applying color typically with either a bowl and brush or with an applicator bottle

4. **Process** – Removing stains and allowing time for the color to develop and deposit

5. **Test** – Removing color product from select strands to ensure it has thoroughly and evenly processed prior to rinsing

6. **Remove and Condition** – Following manufacturer's directions to remove color products from the hair and condition

» Additional factors to consider when coloring hair include the effects design principles can have on the sculpture:

■ Solid form
■ Graduated form
■ Increase-layered form
■ Uniformly layered form

110ᶜ.8 |
COLOR
GUEST EXPERIENCE

EXPLORE //

**Beyond great color
formulation and
application skills, how
can you ensure that your
clients return and choose
you over someone else?**

» INSPIRE //

Providing an exceptional guest experience, in addition to solid hair-coloring skills, can be your success formula to quickly growing a loyal clientele.

ACHIEVE //

Following this lesson on *Color Guest Experience*, you'll be able to:

>> Summarize the service essentials as they relate to color services

>> Discuss examples of infection control and safety guidelines for color services

FOCUS //

COLOR GUEST EXPERIENCE

Color Service Essentials

Color Infection Control and Safety

In a competitive salon environment, one thing that can set you apart is your guest relations. A guest that comes in for a service and leaves with a smile on their face is a testimony to how a stylist can change a person's day. This ability will not only make your clients feel good but will gain you their appreciation and loyalty, in addition to referrals.

110^c.8 |
COLOR GUEST EXPERIENCE

The guest experience begins with building rapport and trust with your client. A key factor for a successful color service is clear communication. Communicating with your client prior to the color service will ensure predictable results that match your client's expectations and needs and helps avoid any misunderstandings. Hair color swatches, magazines and pictures can be used as guides while consulting with the client to reinforce communication.

» COLOR SERVICE ESSENTIALS

To avoid a false color analysis, be sure the area is well lit. Proper lighting in the hair color area is essential for an accurate analysis, color selection, application and final evaluation. Keep in mind:

» Incandescent lighting generally makes hair appear warmer

» Fluorescent lighting makes hair appear cooler

» Fluorescent lighting can be balanced for daylight, creating a more natural light reflection

Practice reflective listening skills by listening closely and then repeating what your client has said to you to avoid any misunderstandings.

CONNECT

>> Meet and greet the client with a firm handshake and a pleasant tone of voice.

>> Communicate to build rapport and develop a relationship with the client.

CONSULT

>> Ask questions to discover information about past color services and to gain insight into your client's wants and needs. Start with open-ended questions, such as: "What made you become interested in a color service today?"

>> Ask about clothing, makeup preferences and lifestyle.

>> Ask your clients about maintaining the new color, and make them aware of the financial commitment.

>> Analyze face and body shape, physical features, eyes and skin tone.

>> Analyze the porosity and condition of the hair, since you want to always maintain the best possible condition of the hair.

>> Assess the facts and thoroughly think through your recommendations by visualizing the end result.

- ▪ Use photos, magazines and/or hair color swatches to better understand your client's desires.

- ▪ Don't be afraid to let your client know if it's not advisable to perform a service.

- ▪ Remember, not all requests are possible, even on healthy hair.

>> Explain your recommended solutions and the cost for the initial and upkeep services.

>> If the client seems hesitant about your recommendation, ask additional questions related to the client's desired outcome.

>> Gain feedback and consent from your client before proceeding with the service.

CREATE

>> Ensure client is protected by draping them with towels and a cape appropriate for a chemical service.

>> Ensure client comfort during the service, repeatedly checking for possible scalp irritation or staining of the skin.

>> Stay focused on delivering the color service to the best of your ability.

>> Keep your client informed with brief explanations on what you're doing and the products used.

>> Produce a functional, predictable and pleasing result.

>> If client is seated under a hood dryer, check on them frequently.

- ▪ Adjust the heat settings, as needed.

- ▪ Offer reading materials.

>> Teach the client how to perform at-home color care maintenance.

COMPLETE

>> Reinforce the client's satisfaction with the overall experience.

>> Make professional product recommendations to maintain the appearance and condition of your client's hair color, such as shampoos and conditioners.

>> Invite your client to make a retail purchase for home care.

>> Prebook – Suggest a future appointment for your client's next visit.

>> End guest's visit with a warm and personal goodbye.

>> Discard single-use supplies, disinfect tools and arrange workstation.

>> Wash your hands.

>> Update the client's record with accurate information for future services as well as retail recommendations.

>> Provide follow-up after the salon visit.

Refer to the lessons on the four Service Essentials and *Color Design* for additional guidelines.

CLIENT RECORD/RELEASE FORM

CLIENT CHEMICAL COLOR RECORD

Date	Formula	Product	Process Time	Patch Test	Strand Test
				☐ Negative ☐ Positive Remarks:	☐ Good ☐ Poor ☐ Too Light ☐ Too Dark Remarks:

Description of Hair:

Length	Density	Texture	Porosity	Natural Hair Color	Desired Hair Color
• Short	• Light	• Fine	• Average	• Level (1-10)	• Level (1-10)
• Medium	• Medium	• Medium	• Resistant	• Tone (warm, cool, etc.)	• Tone (warm, cool, etc.)
• Long	• Heavy	• Coarse	• Extreme	• Intensity: Mild, Medium, Strong	• Intensity: Mild, Medium, Strong

Condition: ☐ Dry   ☐ Oily   ☐ Faded   ☐ Streaked   ☐ % Gray

Medications: _____

Vitamins: _____

Comments: _____

_____

_____

_____

Price of Service: _____

Signature of Student: Signature of Instructor:

_____   _____

One key contributor to successful client relationships is to keep accurate records. The client record contains information, such as:

>> Client's contact information

>> Color formulation and products

>> Information about the client's hair and scalp

>> Application methods and processing time

>> Considerations for the next visit

The client record is used throughout the salon visit, from the consultation period, until the client has left the salon.

CLIENT CHEMICAL COLOR RELEASE FORM

Name: _____   Phone Number: _____

Address: _____   City, State, Zip: _____

I request a Bleach, Toner, Tint (circle one), and I fully understand that this service is to be given by a student of cosmetology at Your Name Beauty School. I hereby express my willingness for a student to do this work. I, furthermore, understand that I will assume full responsibility thereof.

Your Name Beauty School

Witness: _____   Client Signature: _____

Date: _____   Date: _____

A client release statement helps the school or salon owner avoid retribution as a result of any damages or accidents and may be required as part of some malpractice insurance policies.

>> It's not a legal document

>> It may not absolve the colorist from responsibility for damage that may occur
to the client's hair as a result of the chemical service

SALONCONNECTION

Client Record Systems

Nowadays, most salons don't use physical cards to house client information. Instead, all the information is entered into the salon's computer system. This is beneficial in regards to always having access to the previous services, instead of what fits on a card. You, as the stylist, don't have to worry about losing cards, and if the client has their hair done by another stylist at the salon, you'll know what they used, as well.

COLOR COMMUNICATION GUIDELINES

Many times, clients will not ask directly to have a color service done. As a stylist, you need to listen for cues that offer you an opportunity to recommend a color service. The following are a few cues that you might hear from a client during the consultation or at any point during the service. Sample responses that promote client trust, open communication and encourage a client to entrust you with their hair color are offered as suggestions.

CLIENT CUE	DESIGNER RESPONSE
"I'm really starting to get tired of my gray hair! But I'm worried coloring it will look unnatural."	"Natural hair colors look natural because they're a blend of many different shades. Natural hair colors also are just a hint lighter around the face and darker in the nape. Some subtle lowlights can blend your gray harmoniously, and the color you'll have will match your complexion and look natural."
"Wow, I really love the new haircut you just gave me. I feel like a different person!"	"I'm so glad you like it. It looks really great on you! Now that your hair has a more distinct shape, imagine how a color could really accentuate it. If we can stay within the warmer color ranges around your face, we can also beautifully brighten your eyes. Let me show you some ideas."
"I can't believe how dark my hair turned now that summer is a few months past, but I hate when I see obvious highlights that look so fake."	"So, you'd like your highlights to look more natural, like lightened by the sun? There are techniques that can make that happen. I can place very subtle highlights to make sure they mimic naturally lightened hair as closely as possible, and I can concentrate them more in areas where the sun would lighten your hair, like around the face and through the top. That way, your hair will look like it's always sun-kissed."
"My scalp has a tendency to burn when I color my hair."	"Thank you for telling me! I always perform a patch test on a new color client to rule out any allergies. Also, many times if you shampoo your hair the same day as a color service, your scalp might tingle, since the natural oils have been removed. In either case, I'll perform a patch test to ensure you're not allergic to the product."
"I loved the color you did last time, but it faded rather quickly, and after a week, it was pretty dull already."	"I'm sorry to hear that. Unfortunately, that can happen with slightly porous hair. Could you remind me what you use for home care? I can recommend some of our color-enhancing shampoos and conditioners that redeposit color pigment, while keeping your hair healthy and your color looking fresh between visits."
"I would love for my curly hair to be a bit lighter but don't want an all-over color that would give me roots to maintain. I tried highlights before, but quite honestly, they looked like cooked spaghetti in my dark hair. I'm not sure what I should do..."	"I understand that must have been frustrating. There are a couple of options: 1. We can go with highlights, but they'll need to be finer and won't really show up as highlights, but they will very much blend in and give a lighter effect. 2. Another option would be to gently lighten the ends of your hair only and following that with a shine enhancing rinse. That will help your color look lighter and brighter and also requires only a little upkeep."

DISCOVER**MORE**

Promoting Hair Color Services

Credibility is key to effective communication. To build credibility with clients, you should speak from experience regarding the services and products you're recommending. Focus more on communicating the value or benefit the client will gain from the hair color service using current, professional terminology. Examples of professional terminology include:

>> Lighten (versus bleach)

>> Color (versus dye)

>> Highlighting or weaving (versus frosting or streaking)

>> Sun-kissed ends (versus bleached ends)

>> Deepen (versus making darker)

>> Adding richness and shine (versus toning or dyeing)

COLOR INFECTION CONTROL AND SAFETY

It is your responsibility to protect your client by following infection control and safety guidelines with any and all services you provide.

Cleaning is a process of removing dirt, debris and potential pathogens to aid in slowing the growth of pathogens. Cleaning is performed prior to disinfection procedures.

Disinfection methods kill certain pathogens (bacteria, viruses and fungi) with the exception of spores. Disinfectants are available in varied forms, including concentrate, liquid, spray or wipes that are approved EPA-registered disinfectants available for use in the salon industry. Immersion, and the use of disinfecting spray or wipes are common practices when it comes to disinfecting tools, multi-use supplies and equipment in the salon. Be sure to follow the manufacturer's directions for mixing disinfecting solutions and contact time, if applicable.

COLOR SERVICE SAFETY PRECAUTIONS

The following is a list of safety precautions that you should always adhere to prior to and during a color service to protect the client and yourself.

1. Practice infection control guidelines, including disinfection procedures. Protect yourself by wearing a colorist apron and gloves and by washing your hands before and after each client visit.

2. Perform a patch test 24 to 48 hours prior to the application of an aniline derivative tint. See "Predisposition (Skin Patch) Test" in this lesson.

3. Perform the color service only if the patch test is negative and there are no metallic or compound dyes present.

4. Protect the client's clothing with proper draping. See "Draping for a Color Service" in this lesson.

5. Check for scalp abrasions. Do not proceed with the service if there are any cuts or irritations.

6. Perform a preliminary strand test and subsequent strand tests as needed. See "Strand Tests" later in this lesson.

7. Do not brush hair prior to a color service; doing so will irritate the scalp.

8. If pre-shampooing is necessary, use light massage movements and tepid (lukewarm) water.

9. Use disinfected applicator bottles, brushes and combs. Only use plastic or glass bowls to mix the color formula.

10. Once the formula is mixed, use it immediately. Discard any leftover product once the service is completed.

11. Do not allow the product to come in contact with eyes. If it does, rinse the eyes immediately with tepid water, and refer the client to a physician.

12. Monitor the color process to assess color development and to prevent any stress to the skin, scalp or hair. If the client experiences discomfort, remove the product immediately.

13. During a retouch color service, avoid overlapping the product, especially with lightener, as this may cause breakage.

14. Avoid leaving the client unattended during a color service.

15. Never color hair that has been colored with a product that contains metallic salts. See "Test for Metallic Salts" in the *Nonoxidative Color Products* lesson.

16. Rinse the hair with lukewarm or cool water.

17. Do not use aniline derivative tints to color eyelashes or eyebrows; if product enters the eyes, it may cause blindness.

18. Complete the client record, noting any allergies or adverse reactions the client may have experienced.

Draping for a Color Service

Proper draping is required to protect a client's skin and clothing during hair color services. Prior to draping the client, ask the client to remove neck jewelry, earrings and eyeglasses and store them in a safe place. To perform a proper draping procedure for a color service, you will need two towels and a plastic cape.

DRAPING GUIDELINES FOR A COLOR SERVICE

>> Wash hands

>> Have client remove jewelry; store in a secure place

>> Clip client's hair out of the way

>> Cross towel over client's shoulders

>> Position cape over towel and fasten

>> Drape a second towel over cape

>> Detangle the hair and section according to the applicable service; avoid brushing the scalp

>> Apply barrier cream to entire hairline to prevent irritation and staining

>> Clean work area

Predisposition (Skin Patch) Test

According to the U.S. Federal Food, Drug, and Cosmetic Act, **all color products containing an aniline derivative ingredient require a predisposition (skin patch) test 24 to 48 hours prior to the hair color service.** This test will help determine if the client is sensitive or allergic to certain chemicals in the hair color product.

Once the predisposition test has been performed, it is important to analyze the results. If the results are:

>> **Negative (no reaction), the color formula may safely be used**

>> **Positive (reaction), do not proceed with the service and have the client seek medical assistance; the results can include any of the following:**
- **Redness**
- **Swelling**
- **Blisters**
- **Itching**
- **Burning of the skin**
- **Respiratory distress**

Remember your knowledge on non-oxidative and oxidative color products and always follow manufacturers' directions and read Safety Data Sheets (SDS).

Predisposition (Skin Patch) Test Guidelines

INSIDE ELBOW	BACK OF EAR	
		CLEANSE AREA » Wash your hands » Put on gloves » Cleanse test area
		APPLY INTENDED FORMULA » Apply intended formula with cotton swab » Leave undisturbed for 24 hours
		CHECK FOR RESULTS » Analyze results; determine if reaction is negative (no signs) or positive (signs of redness, swelling, blisters, itching or burning of the skin and/or respiratory distress) » If reaction is negative, proceed with service; if reaction is positive, do not proceed with service » Record results in client record » Clean work area

Strand Tests

A strand test is the process of isolating a section of hair for analysis.

>> **Preliminary strand test**
   ▪ **Performed 24 to 48 hours before hair color service to determine proper color formulation**

   ▪ Can be performed immediately following a negative predisposition test: important factors you'll discover from a strand test and analyzing the results prior to service include:
     • Correct formula and processing time
     • Reaction of the hair and what particular procedures may be needed to ensure color absorption (conditioning, filling, etc.)
     • Presence of coating on the hair from previous applications that could be damaging or undesirable (metallic, henna, product build-up, etc.)

   ▪ The intended formula is mixed and applied to a section of hair that is concealed but still viewable for the client

   ▪ May be repeated to achieve the desired result

>> **Color development strand test**
   ▪ **Performed during the color processing to monitor processing time and assess any stress on the hair or scalp**

COLOR DEVELOPMENT STRAND TEST (DURING SERVICE) GUIDELINES

Strand testing during the processing time of the color service allows you to monitor color development and check for stress to the hair and scalp. You should perform strand tests in several areas, such as the most resistant area, and the area of the initial application. To perform a color development strand test, you'll need a water bottle and white towel.

>> Select a small section of hair

>> Position the selected strand on a towel

>> Spray water along the strand

>> Gently rub across the strand to remove the product thoroughly

>> Check results against a white towel

>> Desirable results: Shampoo and condition the hair

>> Undesirable results: Continue processing until proper results are achieved

PRELIMINARY STRAND TEST GUIDELINES

>> Wash your hands

>> Analyze skin patch test results; if negative, proceed with preliminary strand test

>> Drape client for chemical service

>> Wear protective gloves and colorist apron

>> Isolate a small section of hair visible to client

>> Apply the intended color formula

>> Set timer

>> Rinse out color product from test strand at the end of the processing time; shampoo, rinse and dry

>> Analyze results and make any necessary color formula adjustments; perform another strand test, if appropriate

>> Document results

>> Clean color service area

CLEANING AND DISINFECTION GUIDELINES

Keep in mind that only nonporous tools, supplies and equipment can be disinfected. All single-use items must be discarded after each use. Always follow your area's regulatory guidelines.

TOOLS, SUPPLIES AND EQUIPMENT	CLEANING GUIDELINES	DISINFECTION GUIDELINES
Color Bowl	Preclean with soap and water.	Use an approved EPA-registered disinfectant solution or spray.
Applicator Bottle	Preclean with soap and water.	Use an approved EPA-registered disinfectant solution or spray.
Color Brush	Remove hair and debris. Preclean with soap and water. Dry thoroughly.	Use an approved EPA-registered disinfectant solution or spray.
Combs	Remove hair and debris. Preclean with soap and water.	Immerse in an approved EPA-registered disinfectant solution.
Clips	Preclean with soap and water.	Immerse in an approved EPA-registered disinfectant solution.
Cape	Remove hair and color product from cape. Wash in washing machine with soap after each use.	Some regulatory agencies may require use of an approved EPA-registered disinfectant.
Towels	Remove hair from towels. Wash in washing machine with soap after each use.	Some regulatory agencies may require use of an approved EPA-registered disinfectant.

Store disinfected tools and multi-use supplies in a clean, dry, covered container or cabinet.

Alert!

If tools, multi-use supplies or equipment have come in contact with blood or body fluids, the following disinfection procedures must take place:

Use an approved EPA-registered hospital disinfectant according to manufacturer's directions and as required by your area's regulatory agency.

CARE AND SAFETY

Follow infection control procedures for personal care and client safety guidelines before and during the color service to ensure your safety and the clients', while also contributing to the salon care.

Personal Care	Client Care Prior to the Service	Client Care During the Service	Salon Care
>> Check that your personal standards of health and hygiene minimize the spread of infection.	>> Perform a skin test 24 to 48 hours prior to the application of an aniline derivative product.	>> If pre-shampooing is necessary, use light massage movements and tepid (lukewarm) water.	>> Follow health and safety guidelines, including cleaning and disinfecting guidelines.
>> Wash hands and dry thoroughly with a single-use towel.	>> Protect the client's skin and clothing from color stains by draping them with a towel for a color service.	>> Protect the client's skin by applying barrier cream around the hairline and ears.	>> Ensure equipment, including the salon chair, is clean and disinfected.
>> Minimize fatigue by maintaining good posture during the service.	>> Check the scalp for any diseases or disorders. If any are evident, refer client to a physician; do not proceed with the service.	>> Do not permit the product to come in contact with the eyes. If it does, rinse the eyes immediately with tepid water.	>> Promote a professional image by ensuring your workstation is clean and tidy throughout the service.
>> Refer to your area's regulatory agency for proper mixing/handling of disinfectant solutions.	>> Clean and disinfect tools appropriately.	>> Be sure the cape stays in place, and the client's arms are underneath the cape.	>> Use clean and disinfected applicator bottles, brushes and combs; use only plastic or glass bowls to mix color.
>> Wear protective single-use or multi-use gloves.	>> Be sure the cape stays in place, and the client's arms are underneath the cape.	>> Monitor the color service, and perform a strand test, as needed, to check color development.	>> Use mixed products immediately; discard any leftover product once the service is complete.
>> If any tools are dropped on the floor, pick them up then clean and disinfect.		>> Check in, and ask client about any scalp sensitivity or irritations.	>> Refer to SDS.
>> Disinfect workstation.		>> Disinfect workstation.	
		>> Complete or update the client record noting the formula, processing time and any sensitivities experienced.	

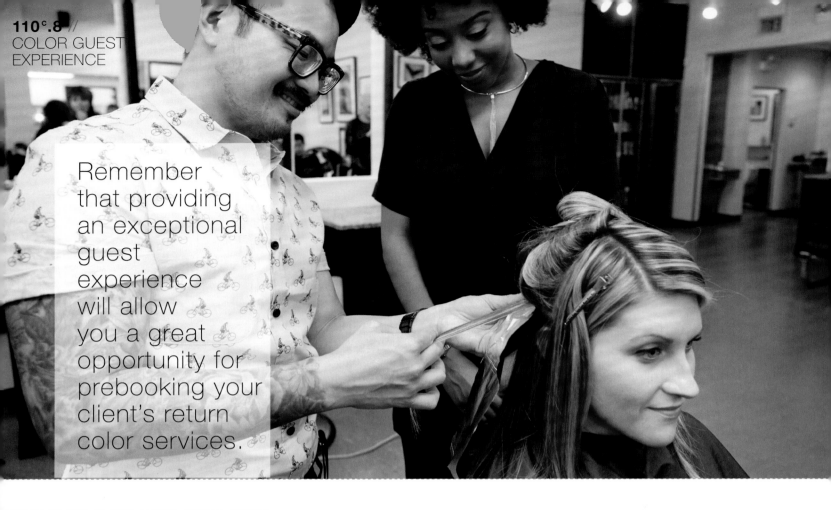

Remember that providing an exceptional guest experience will allow you a great opportunity for prebooking your client's return color services.

LESSONS LEARNED

The service essentials related to hair color can be summarized, as follows:

» Connect – Meet and greet clients and communicate to build rapport

» Consult – Ask questions to discover client needs; analyze client's face, body shape, physical features, hair and scalp; explain recommended solutions, and gain feedback and consent to move forward

» Create – Ensure client safety and comfort; stay focused to deliver the best service; explain process and products to your client; teach the client at-home care maintenance

» Complete – Request specific feedback; recommend home-care products; suggest future appointment times; complete client record

Infection control and safety guidelines must be followed throughout a color service to ensure your safety and the safety of the clients and the salon. Disinfectants are available in varied forms including concentrate, liquid, spray or wipes that have EPA approval for use in the salon industry. Be guided by your area's regulatory agency for proper cleaning and disinfection guidelines.

110ᶜ.9 //
COLOR
SERVICE

EXPLORE //

Have you ever experienced a color service that didn't turn out exactly the way you hoped?

INSPIRE //

Performing accurate color application procedures ensures that the color design you set out to achieve indeed becomes a reality.

Service procedures ensure the well-being and care of clients by providing the framework for your color service execution. This lesson is a culmination of everything you've learned about color theory, design, products, tools, skills and guest relations; it's where you apply your knowledge before, during and after the color service to ensure client safety and satisfaction.

ACHIEVE //

Following this lesson on *Color Service*, you'll be able to:

>> Provide examples of procedural guidelines to follow when performing a hair color service

>> Describe the three areas of color service

>> Differentiate application methods for various hair color products

>> Restate solutions to common hair color problems

>> Explain the guidelines for returning a client to their natural hair color

FOCUS //

COLOR SERVICE

Color Client Guidelines

Color Product Overview

Color Service Overview

Hair Color Problems
and Solutions

Tint Back Guidelines

Hair Color Removal Techniques

Color Rubric

110ᶜ.9 | COLOR SERVICE

By understanding the following color service procedures, you'll know how to change your clients' hair color, allowing you the opportunity to create an array of color designs for a wide variety of client needs.

COLOR CLIENT GUIDELINES

Client-centered guidelines help you do everything possible to enhance your client's comfort and satisfaction. Combining your experience with predictable color results and client-centered guidelines will ensure exceptional color results and a pleasant experience for your clients.

The following chart will help you ensure your client's comfort and safety during the color service.

SECTION		» Explain that you're using a sectioning pattern that is specifically designated to achieve desired results. » Consider the sculpture, texture and position of weight and volume. » Consider natural growth patterns and density, and adjust sections if needed.
PART		» Explain to the client how the direction and width of the parting will affect the color results.
APPLY		» Work neatly and accurately, so the client doesn't have to worry about stains on the skin, color "bleeding" or overlapping colors. » Your neatness and proficiency demonstrate confidence and efficiency to your clients, and puts them at ease.
PROCESS		» Maintain client comfort by ensuring the cape is on the outside back of the chair and draping is secure. » Inform the client of the approximate processing time. » Remove color from skin around the hairline to prevent staining. » Offer beverage or reading material to the client while processing. » Check on clients during processing, so they won't feel forgotten.
TEST		» Explain to the client that you're ensuring the color has developed successfully prior to rinsing. » Perform a strand test in various areas of the design, especially when working on hair with different degrees of porosity.
REMOVE AND CONDITION		» Ensure the client's neck is comfortably positioned in the shampoo bowl while rinsing. » Avoid strong massage movements, since the scalp may be sensitive, and ask client if water temperature is comfortable. » Position your hand to shield the client's face and ears while rinsing. » Inform clients of the importance of at-home care.

COLOR PRODUCT OVERVIEW

This portion of the lesson gives a brief overview of the hair color products you'll use most often in the salon. Being familiar with these products prepares you for the many hair color service possibilities you'll encounter in the salon.

HAIR COLOR PRODUCTS

CATEGORY	FUNCTION	LASTING POWER	APPLICATION METHOD
NONOXIDATIVE (not mixed with developer)			
Temporary	Deposits color	From shampoo to shampoo	Base to ends at shampoo bowl; combed on
Semi-permanent	Deposits color; adds shine; cannot lighten hair	4 to 6 shampoos; fades with each shampoo	Base to ends (heat may be required)
OXIDATIVE (mixed with developer)			
Demi-permanent	Deposits color, but usually does not lighten hair	Fades in 6 to 8 weeks	Base to ends (darker result)
		New growth 6 to 8 weeks	Base only
Permanent (also known as single-process tints)	Lightens and deposits color	Permanent	Base to ends (darker result) Midstrand to porous ends, then base and ends (lighter result)
		New growth 3 to 6 weeks	Base only
LIGHTENERS (mixed with developer)			
On-the-scalp	Lightens existing hair color (can be used on scalp)	Permanent	Midstrand to porous ends, then base and ends (lighter result)
		New growth in 3 to 6 weeks	Base only
Off-the-scalp	Lightens existing hair color (used off the scalp for special effects, i.e., highlighting, painting, etc.)	Permanent	Slightly away from the scalp to the ends (lighter result)
		New growth 3 to 6 weeks or longer depending on color design	Base only

COLOR SERVICE OVERVIEW

The Color Service Overview identifies the three areas of all color services:

>> Color Preparation provides a brief overview of the steps to follow before you actually begin the color design.

>> Color Procedure provides an overview of the procedures you'll use during the color design to ensure predictable results.

>> Color Completion provides an overview of the steps to follow after performing the color design to ensure guest satisfaction.

SERVICE ESSENTIALS: THE FOUR CS
The Color Procedure includes attention to the Four Cs.

1. **CONNECT**
   Establishes rapport and builds credibility with each client

2. **CONSULT**
   Analyzes client wants and needs, visualizes the end result, organizes the plan for follow-through and obtains client agreement

3. **CREATE**
   Produces functional, predictable and pleasing results

4. **COMPLETE**
   Reviews the service experience and client satisfaction, offers product recommendations, expresses appreciation and provides follow-up

COLOR PROCEDURES OVERVIEW

Understanding the following color guidelines and procedures will allow you to create an endless array of hair color designs for your clients.

This section contains guidelines specifically for:
>> Applying nonoxidative temporary rinse
>> Applying semi-permanent color

Followed by procedural overviews, which review the preparation, procedure and completion phases for:
>> Oxidative darker result
>> Oxidative lighter result
>> Double-process blond

The basic steps for a color procedure include:
>> Section
>> Part
>> Apply
>> Test
>> Remove and condition

Note: Removing may or may not include shampooing depending on manufacturer's directions.

Nonoxidative Temporary Color Guidelines

Temporary colors are usually applied to clean, towel-blotted hair and remain on the hair until the next shampoo. These colors are generally applied at the shampoo bowl with an applicator bottle because of their liquid consistency. Read the manufacturer's directions for application procedures. Listed below are general guidelines for a temporary color rinse application.

>> Wash and sanitize hands.

>> Gather and assemble color essentials.

>> Wear protective gloves and apron.

>> Drape client for color service.

>> Shampoo and towel-blot hair thoroughly.

>> Apply color with an applicator bottle from scalp to ends for all-over coverage, or comb the color on for a blended effect.

>> Blot excess color to prevent dripping; do not rinse the hair.

>> Style the hair as desired.

>> Record the results in the client's record; organize materials.

>> Clean workspace.

Nonoxidative Semi-Permanent Color Guidelines

For application and processing procedures, read manufacturer's directions, which may vary. Application timing for semi-permanent color shouldn't exceed 15 minutes.

>> Section the hair into four areas.

>> Apply barrier cream.

>> Pour color into bottle.

>> Outline sectioning lines in back.

>> Take 1" (2.5 cm) horizontal partings.

>> Apply color from base to midstrand, omitting porous ends.

>> Complete first section working from top to nape.

>> Complete back sections.

>> Outline side sections, apply color to these sections from diagonal-back partings.

>> Apply color to remaining midstrand and ends.

>> Work color through for even saturation.

>> Apply cotton around hairline.

>> Place plastic cap over hair.

>> Position client under pre-heated dryer, if applicable.

>> Set timer.

>> Perform strand test to check color.

>> Rinse, shampoo and remove any color stains.

>> Condition and finish hair, as desired.

>> Clean work area.

OXIDATIVE COLOR: DARKER RESULT SERVICE OVERVIEW

When applying an oxidative color for a darker result, color is applied from base to ends. If the ends are porous, you may apply a filler to them first or delay application of color to the porous ends. This application technique is also called a virgin darker when it's performed for the first time. Retouches are applied to the base area only. If the previously colored hair has faded, demi-permanent colors in a matching or slightly lighter tone can be applied to refresh the color.

PREPARATION	>> Perform predisposition test 24 to 48 hours before service; if negative, proceed with hair color service. >> Disinfect color area. >> Arrange disinfected tools and supplies, including color bowl, color brush, gloves, large-tooth comb, tail comb, sectioning clips, hair color, developer and barrier cream. >> Wash hands; drape client for color service; perform hair and scalp analysis; wear protective gloves and color apron; perform preliminary strand test. >> Review previous client record, if applicable.

PROCEDURE	>> Apply barrier cream around hairline and ears.
	>> **Section** hair into four sections.
	>> Measure and mix color formula.
	>> Outline first back section.
	>> **Part** hair using ¼" (.6 cm) horizontal partings across back sections.
	>> **Apply** color from base to end; work from the nape upward to top of section.
	   ▪ Complete the section following the same procedures, and bring hair down.
	   ▪ Repeat on the other back section.
	>> **Apply** color to remaining front sections using diagonal-back partings; work from top down; subdivide for control.
	   ▪ Reapply around hairline ensuring coverage; bring hair down.
	   ▪ Cross-check application.
	   ▪ Remove color stains on the skin.
	>> **Process** color according to manufacturer's instructions.
	>> Perform a strand **test** to check color development.
	>> Rinse and shampoo to **remove** color from hair and skin; **condition.**
	>> Style the hair.

RETOUCH GUIDELINES	Depending on how fast your client's hair grows and the color product used, retouches are generally performed every 3 to 6 weeks. >> Apply color to the new growth only. >> Do not overlap onto previously colored hair. >> If previously colored hair has faded, apply a demi-permanent color in a matching or slightly lighter shade to restore vibrancy. This may be referred to as color glazing.

* For Completion steps, see page 127.

OXIDATIVE COLOR: LIGHTER RESULT SERVICE OVERVIEW

When lightening hair for the first time (virgin technique), the color is applied first from the midstrand up to the porous ends. The color is applied to the base last, since the lightening action is accelerated due to:

>> Incomplete keratinization of the new growth.

>> Additional body heat at the base area.

Very porous ends may also process faster requiring less processing time. Retouch applications are only applied to the new growth and not overlapped onto the previously lightened hair.

PREPARATION	>> Perform predisposition test 24 to 48 hours before service; if negative, proceed with hair color service. >> Disinfect color area. >> Arrange disinfected tools and supplies, including color bowl, color brush, gloves, large-tooth comb, tail comb, sectioning clips, hair color, developer and barrier cream. >> Wash hands; drape client for color service; perform hair and scalp analysis; wear protective gloves and color apron; perform preliminary strand test. >> Review previous client record, if applicable.

PROCEDURE	>> **Section** hair into four sections; apply barrier cream around hairline.
	>> Measure and mix formula.
	>> Begin the application in the most resistant area; **part** using ¼" (.6 cm) partings, and **apply** the color ½" (1.25 cm) away from the scalp on both sides of the strand out to the porous ends; if the ends are not porous, apply color through to the ends.
	   ▪ Repeat the same application on remaining sections, working from the top of the section to the bottom.
	   ▪ Cross-check to ensure even coverage and set timer.
	>> **Process** according to manufacturer's instructions.
	>> Perform a color development strand **test.**
	>> Apply newly mixed color to the base and ends when the hair has reached 50% of the desired level, using the same parting pattern.
	>> Set timer and perform development strand test.
	>> **Remove** color, rinse thoroughly when hair has reached desired level; remove color stains around hairline; shampoo and **condition** hair.
	>> Style the hair.

RETOUCH GUIDELINES	New growth on lighter hair: >> Is more visible. >> Requires more frequent retouches, typically every 3 to 6 weeks. Color is applied to the base area, avoiding the previously colored hair. If the previously colored hair has faded, apply a demi-permanent product in a matching or lighter tone to refresh the color. 

* For Completion steps, see page 127.

DOUBLE-PROCESS SERVICE OVERVIEW

A double-process technique is a two-step process that involves lightening the hair (decolorization) first, then recolorizing to the desired tone.

For the decolorization step keep in mind:

>> Generally ⅛" (.3 cm) horizontal partings are used throughout for even product penetration.

>> **First apply lightener ½" (1.25 cm) away from the scalp out to the porous ends.**

>> Next, process until hair has reached approximately 50% of the desired lightness.

>> Then, apply a fresh mixture to the base.

>> If the ends are very porous, delay the application of the lightener until after the base application.

PREPARATION	>> Perform predisposition test 24 to 48 hours before service, if applicable, for toner application. >> Disinfect color area. >> Arrange disinfected tools and supplies, including color bowl, color brush, gloves, large-tooth comb, tail comb, sectioning clips, on-the-scalp lightener, developer, toner and barrier cream. >> Wash hands; drape client for color service; perform hair and scalp analysis; wear protective gloves and color apron; perform preliminary strand test. >> Review previous client record, if applicable.
PROCEDURE	>> **Section** the hair into four sections. ▪ Apply barrier cream around entire hairline. ▪ Begin at the back crown or most resistant area. >> Decolorize the hair. ▪ **Part** hair using ⅛" (.3 cm) horizontal partings. ▪ Apply lightener ½" (1.25 cm) away from scalp through ends on both sides of the strand; if ends are porous, delay application of lightener until after base application. ▪ **Apply** lightener generously, subdividing partings while working from the top of the section to the bottom; complete section. ▪ Place cotton at base between each parting to prevent seepage. ▪ Repeat same procedure in next back section. ▪ Part along slight diagonal-back partings on front side to keep lightener away from client's face, and repeat same application procedures as in back. ▪ Work from the top to the bottom of each front section using the same application procedures; bring each parting down. ▪ **Process** while monitoring for desired degree of decolorization. ▪ Perform a strand **test** for desired degree of decolorization, removing the lightener with a damp towel to see results clearly. ▪ Apply lightener to base when hair has decolorized halfway to desired degree of lightness by removing cotton and using same parting pattern used previously. ▪ Apply product around hairline. ▪ Cross-check using a parting pattern opposite the initial application to ensure even coverage. ▪ Keep lightener moist during processing time by reapplying freshly mixed product, as necessary. ▪ Process until an even degree of lightness is achieved from base to ends. ▪ **Remove** lightener from hair and scalp rinsing thoroughly, then shampoo and towel-dry hair; check to ensure there are no scalp abrasions.

DOUBLE-PROCESS SERVICE OVERVIEW (CONT'D)

PROCEDURE (CONT'D)

>>> Recolorize the hair.
  - ▧ Mix toner formula.
  - ▧ **Section** hair for toner application with same pattern previously used.
  - ▧ Outline each section, then **part** the hair, and **apply** toner from base to ends working from top to bottom of each section.
  - ▧ Outline hairline for even coverage.
  - ▧ **Process** according to manufacturer's directions.
>> Rinse and shampoo to **remove** toner and **condition** hair.
>> Finish color design.

OPTIONAL PROCEDURE

>> An alternate application method for the double-process technique includes beginning at the nape and working upward, while applying lightener to one side of the strand only.

RETOUCH GUIDELINES

Retouch applications:
>> Performed every 3 to 6 weeks, depending on the rate of new growth and degree of contrast.
>> **Lightener is applied to the new growth only.**
>> Use ⅛" (.3 cm) partings to ensure consistent application.
>> **Do not overlap the lightener onto the previously treated hair, since this may cause overprocessing and breakage.**
>> Decolorize the new growth to the same degree as the previously lightened hair to ensure an even color.
>> Once the lightener is shampooed from the hair, towel dry the hair and apply toner to the new growth.
  - ▧ If the midstrands and ends need refreshing, distribute a diluted color formula throughout the remaining lengths during the last few minutes of processing.

* For Completion steps, see next page.

REMINDER
With a virgin double-process technique, the lightener isn't applied immediately to the base, because the body heat and incomplete keratinization near the scalp will cause the hair to lighten more quickly there, resulting in an uneven color formula.

COMPLETION	>> Reinforce client's satisfaction with the overall experience.
	>> Make professional product recommendations.
	>> Prebook client's next appointment.
	>> End client's visit with warm and personal goodbye.
	>> Discard non-reusable materials, disinfect tools and arrange workstation in proper order.
	>> Wash your hands.
	>> Complete client record.

SALONCONNECTION

Color Dilution

How do colorists dilute their formulas? They add a clear color to the formula. This keeps the same tones in the formula yet dilutes them, similar to using water to dilute juice. Keep the following in mind; if you add 50% clear to your formula, it will be 50% diluted or less concentrated than the original formula.

While toning after a decolorization, DO NOT leave the client's side. Toners may process extremely fast on freshly lightened hair. Quick application and close monitoring are key to achieve the desired tonal results.

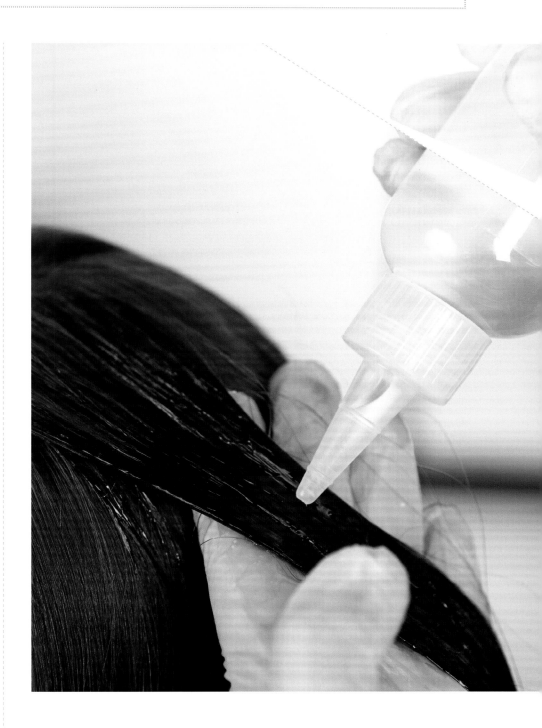

HAIR COLOR PROBLEMS AND SOLUTIONS

The following are a few problems that may occur as part of a hair color service, along with some possible solutions.

THE COLOR FADED QUICKLY

Cause: Uneven porosity due to repeated pulling through of oxidative color through the lengths
Solution: Choose a deposit-only color, such as a demi-permanent, when necessary to refresh the midstrand and ends. The larger molecules will better adhere to the porous strands and not cause any additional porosity over time.

Cause: Harsh cleansing shampoos used during at-home maintenance
Solution: Recommend a shampoo and conditioner for color-treated hair at the end of each color service.

THE COLOR RESULT IS TOO LIGHT

Note: *If the color result was too light, immediately upon completion of the color service, you may apply a nonoxidative or demi-permanent color throughout.*

Cause: The color formula chosen was too light
Solution: Use your color charts to gain complete clarity on desired color. Then, choose a darker color going forward.

Cause: The strength of the developer was too high
Solution: Use a lower strength when more deposit is desired. Identify how many, if any, levels of lift are needed between the existing and desired color. Refer to the manufacturer's guidelines on the appropriate strength developer for the required level(s) of lift or to simply deposit color.

THE COLOR RESULT IS TOO DARK

Note: *If the hair is too dark immediately upon completion of the color service, you may wish to use the following as a guideline to correct the situation:*

>> *Additional shampooing may remove some of the unwanted pigment.*
>> *If the color is still too dark, adding a few, very fine highlights to add brightness and lightness may be enough.*
>> *In extreme cases, a color remover may be needed.*

Cause: The color formula chosen was too dark
Solution: Use an acidic color remover product to reverse the oxidative color process, and rinse the darker pigments out. Follow manufacturer's instructions exactly. Recolor the hair, but formulate 1-2 levels lighter than desired end color. Hair will turn out darker than the formula applied immediately after an acidic color remover. For future appointments, choose a lighter color; use swatches to determine the existing and desired field; take into consideration the porosity of the hair.

Cause: The developer volume chosen was too low
Solution: Use acidic color remover and recolor hair (see above for more detail). For future appointments, adjust the developer strength according to the lift and deposit desired.

Cause: Improper analysis of the type of porosity was made
Solution: Check the porosity of the hair prior to color application; remember, with extreme porosity, color may, at first, take quite intensely and then gradually fade with each shampoo. Use deep-cleanse shampoo, and if needed, cover with plastic cap and place under a hood dryer. Rinse and deep condition. **For future appointments,** use demi- or semi-permanent color in a slightly lighter shade to refresh the lengths and monitor during processing.

INSUFFICIENT GRAY COVERAGE

Cause: The color selected was too light

Solution: Choose a darker color, as it has a heavier concentration of pigment; remember that very light hair colors, above level 9, contain very little brown or neutral pigment to stain the white hair that is mixed into the overall gray-looking hair. Or choose a natural series designed or recommended by the manufacturer for gray coverage.

Cause: The proper analysis for percentage of gray was not made

Solution: Although an accurate analysis may be difficult, use the following as a guideline:

>> Determine whether the hair looks more or less than 50% gray
>> For higher percentages of gray:
  ▪ Use a lower level than the desired level
  ▪ Add warmth to the formula for a natural effect
  ▪ Pre-pigment using the color product mixed with a little bit of water, and apply to the areas with the most white hair concentration, process for 10 minutes optionally with heat, then proceed with standard color application

>> For small amounts of gray:
  ▪ Do not adjust the formula

Cause: Color was not applied evenly

Solution: Apply color evenly from a consistent parting pattern; cross-check, and always outline the hairline.

THE ENDS ARE TOO DARK

Cause: Color was applied to the ends too soon or when not necessary

Solution: Remove some of the unwanted pigment by re-shampooing the hair. In an extreme case, you may need to use a color remover.

For future appointments delay the application until the last 5 to 15 minutes of the processing time, depending on the porosity of the hair.

In the case of retouch service, apply color to the ends only if they are faded, and reformulate for the ends with a demi-permanent color.

THE ENDS ARE TOO LIGHT

Cause: Color was applied too late to the ends; not enough development time was allowed

Solution: Reformulate using a very low strength of developer, and apply the color to the ends. **For future appointments**, apply the formula sooner or adjust the color formula for deposit only.

Cause: Color application to the lengths was inconsistent

Solution: Properly assess hair density, and use smaller partings when applying to the lengths. Thoroughly check for even product coverage and penetration during processing.

TINT BACK GUIDELINES

Coloring hair back to its natural color is called a "tint back" service. A tint back service utilizes all your coloring skills and knowledge. It typically involves a color filler to provide an even base and replaces any missing primary colors.

When determining whether you apply the filler directly to the hair or whether you mix it into the color formula, consider:

>> Degree of porosity

>> Number of levels to color back to

>> Desired final color result

Follow manufacturer's directions to ensure predictable results. Refer back to "Fillers" for additional information.

TINT BACK GUIDELINES

>> Perform a strand test

>> Subdivide the hair into four sections; apply filler to desired areas

>> Process according to manufacturer's directions

>> Re-section the hair, and apply the color formula from the line of demarcation out to the porous ends

>> Process and strand test for color development; then apply to porous ends; process accordingly

   ■ Note that a diluted color formula may be applied to the remaining hair to blend into the line of demarcation

>> Rinse with lukewarm or tepid water, then shampoo

>> Apply conditioner, rinse and style as desired

>> Record formula and results in client's chemical record; complete the service by recommending at-home maintenance products

>> Disinfect tools, discard single-use supplies and clean work area

HAIR COLOR REMOVAL TECHNIQUES

Products known as color removers and dye solvents are designed to remove artificial pigment. There are two types of color removal products available: those that contain bleach and those that don't.

Occasionally, it may become necessary to remove artificial pigment from the hair. Some reasons for removing artificial pigment may include:

» Repeated overlapped applications of hair color have left the hair too dark, dull or have caused an uneven band of color along the strand

» Client wants to color his or her hair to a lighter shade

» A fashion color was used, but the client now desires a more natural hair color

» Incorrect formulas were used, resulting in unwanted shades

Always read manufacturer's directions. As with most color services, a strand test should be performed to:

» Avoid damaging the hair

» Verify whether the service can be performed

Caution must be exercised during a color removal, since the process can be damaging to the hair. In cases of extreme color build-up or removing color pigments that were added more than 6 weeks prior, it may not be possible to completely remove the artificial pigment for the hair.

Color Removers With Bleach
This common type of color remover product is:

» Mixed with hydrogen peroxide for a stronger effect

» Mixed with distilled water for a milder effect

» Designed to lighten the artificial, as well as the natural pigment of the hair

» Almost always used with a neutralizing toner to manage the warm tones produced

» Very similar to a lightener product, which causes similar dryness and potential damage

Color Removers Without Bleach
A more gentle type of color remover comes with two solutions that need to be mixed together prior to application. These less damaging color removers:

» Create a chemical reduction

» Do not bleach or lighten color pigments

» Reverse the bonding that happened during the original color oxidation

» Break the color molecules into smaller components that can be rinsed out of the hair

» Only remove the artificial pigment

» Leave natural color pigments in tact

» Are effective on oxidative color products

» Cannot fully remove color that is more than 4-6 weeks old

DISCOVERMORE

Color removers without bleach are a savior to many colorists and their distressed clients alike. However, they're not widely popular. Search the Internet to find examples of color removers without bleach, and find out what's available to you as a professional and how exactly these products are to be used.

PERMANENT COLOR REMOVAL GUIDELINES

>> Follow manufacturer's directions regarding shampooing the hair prior to the color removal application

>> Section the hair into four basic sections

>> Mix the product in a glass or plastic bowl

>> Begin the application in the darkest area, and apply the product throughout the four sections

>> Complete the application, and follow manufacturer's instructions for processing

>> Strand test frequently

>> Once the color is removed, rinse the product immediately

>> Gently, but thoroughly shampoo, and rinse all remnants of the product from the hair

>> Towel-dry and analyze the hair; it may be necessary to reapply the color remover product in some areas

>> Once the product has been shampooed out, condition then dry the hair, if applicable

Keep in mind that once the artificial color has been removed, the final hair color has not been achieved. The resulting color serves as the foundation for the final hair color. If no signs of scalp irritation are present:

>> Perform a strand test

>> Use a filler, if needed

>> Choose the appropriate color

Keep in mind that the hair has gone through several chemical services, leaving the hair porous; therefore, a low volume developer mixed with a color formula that is one to two shades lighter than your final desired results is advisable.

Henna Removal Guidelines

Hair coated with the vegetable dye henna is generally not compatible with other hair coloring or chemical services. To remove henna, follow these procedures:

>> Apply 70% alcohol to the hairstrand, avoiding direct contact with the scalp; allow alcohol to remain on the hair for 5 to 7 minutes

>> Apply mineral oil directly over the alcohol, completely saturating each strand from scalp to ends

>> Cover the hair with a plastic cap; place under a pre-heated hooded dryer for 30 minutes

>> Without rinsing, apply concentrated shampoo for oily hair, and massage into the lengths; allow shampoo to remain on the hair for 3 minutes

>> Massage the hair again, then rinse thoroughly with hot, but comfortable water

>> Shampoo again; several shampoos may be necessary

COLOR RUBRIC

A performance rubric is a document that identifies criteria at which levels of performance can be measured objectively. The Color Rubric is an example that an instructor might choose to use for scoring. The Color Rubric is divided into three main areas—Preparation, Procedure and Completion. Each area is further divided into step-by-step procedures to follow to ensure client safety and satisfaction.

COLOR RUBRIC

Allotted Time: 1 Hour, 30 Minutes

Student Name: _____ ID Number: _____

Instructor: _____ Date: _____ Start Time: _____ End Time: _____

COLOR (Live Model) – Each scoring item is marked with either a "Yes" or "No." Each "Yes" counts for one point. Total number of points attainable is 33.

CRITERIA	YES	NO	INSTRUCTOR ASSESSMENT
PREPARATION: Did student...			
1. Set up workstation with properly labeled supplies?	☐	☐	
2. Place disinfected tools and supplies at a visibly clean workstation?	☐	☐	
3. Wash hands?	☐	☐	
Connect: Did student...			
4. Meet and greet client with a welcoming smile and pleasant tone of voice?	☐	☐	
5. Communicate to build rapport and develop a relationship with client?	☐	☐	
6. Refer to client by name throughout service?	☐	☐	
Consult: Did student...			
7. Ask questions to discover client's wants and needs?	☐	☐	
8. Analyze client's hair and scalp and check for any contraindications?	☐	☐	
9. Gain feedback and consent from client before proceeding?	☐	☐	
PROCEDURE: Did student...			
10. Properly drape client and prepare for service?	☐	☐	
11. Ensure client protection and comfort by maintaining cape on outside of chair at all times?	☐	☐	
12. Carry out appropriate shampoo and condition procedures, when applicable?	☐	☐	
13. Use products and supplies economically?	☐	☐	
Create: Did student...			
14. Section hair for control?	☐	☐	
15. Formulate color products correctly for the desired result?	☐	☐	
16. Mix and prepare color products correctly?	☐	☐	
17. Part the hair for the application methods and color service performed?	☐	☐	
18. Apply color neatly and accurately on the appropriate areas of the hairstrand?	☐	☐	
19. Use color tools and supplies accurately and efficiently throughout application?	☐	☐	
20. Check hairline and skin for any color stains and address them immediately?	☐	☐	
21. Process color according to manufacturer's directions?	☐	☐	
22. Strand test to assure proper color development?	☐	☐	
23. Carry out appropriate removal, shampoo and condition procedures?	☐	☐	
24. Practice infection control procedures and safety guidelines throughout service?	☐	☐	
COMPLETION (Complete): Did student...			
25. Ask questions, and look for verbal and nonverbal cues to determine client's level of satisfaction?	☐	☐	
26. Make professional product recommendations?	☐	☐	
27. Ask client to make a future appointment?	☐	☐	
28. End guest's visit with a warm and personal goodbye?	☐	☐	
29. Discard single-use supplies?	☐	☐	
30. Disinfect tools and multi-use supplies; disinfect workstation and arrange in proper order?	☐	☐	
31. Complete service within scheduled time?	☐	☐	
32. Complete client record?	☐	☐	
33. Wash their hands following service?	☐	☐	

COMMENTS: _____

TOTAL POINTS = _____ ÷ 33 = _____ %

Each of the procedural steps used to apply color affects how it turns out. Whether you want it even from base to ends, progressing from darker to lighter or contrasting, following procedural steps will help you ensure your client's satisfaction.

LESSONS LEARNED

» Procedural guidelines to follow when performing a color service to ensure client safety include:

- ■ Sectioning the hair, considering the sculpture, texture and position of weight, while considering the natural growth patterns and density

- ■ Parting direction and the width of the parting effects the color results

- ■ Applying product neatly and accurately to avoid staining the skin and overlapping the hair color

- ■ Processing the color, maintaining client comfort, while removing any color from the skin

- ■ Testing strands in various areas to ensure even coverage

- ■ Removing and conditioning the products from the hair, while also informing clients of the importance of at-home care

» The three areas of a color service include the preparation, procedure and completion:

- ■ Preparation includes greeting the client, arranging workstation and performing a hair and scalp analysis

- ■ Procedure includes following the color procedures, while introducing and/or removing color from the hair.

- ■ Completion includes reinforcing client's satisfaction, making product recommendations, rebooking next appointment and disinfecting workstation

» Hair color application methods vary between virgin darker, virgin lighter and retouch applications, as well as other color products.

» Proper hair analysis and color formulation can avoid many hair color problems or rectify them immediately after the service, as well as prevent them for future services.

» The color service, often referred to as tint back, can be performed to return clients to their natural hair color following the tint back guidelines.

SEMI-PERMANENT

EXPLORE

Do you have a preferred shade of makeup foundation that best suits your natural skin tone? What benefits does it offer you and how might they compare to the benefits of semi-permanent colors?

INSPIRE

Semi-permanent colors are widely used in salons to add shine to natural hair, tone unwanted shades and add temporary fashion shades to lighter hair—which is especially popular with younger clients.

ACHIEVE

Following this *Semi-Permanent Workshop*, you'll be able to:

>> Identify the color procedures related to semi-permanent color applications

>> Demonstrate proper procedures of a semi-permanent color application performed with an applicator bottle

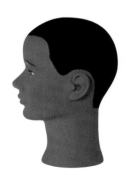

Warm red semi-permanent color adds a tonal change to the natural dark brown level.

A repetition of color is applied throughout the head using an applicator bottle with horizontal partings in the back and diagonal-back partings at the sides.

COLOR DESIGN PROCEDURES

1. SECTION:
   4 sections

2. PART:
   Back – Horizontal | Sides – Diagonal

3. APPLY:
   Base to ends

4. PROCESS:
   Manufacturer's instructions

5. TEST: Strand test

6. REMOVE AND CONDITION:
   Manufacturer's instructions

DESIGN DECISIONS CHART

SEMI-PERMANENT

Draw or fill in the boxes with the appropriate answers.

DESIGN DECISIONS

EXISTING/DESIRED LEVEL

E E E E E

D D D D D

FORM/TEXTURE

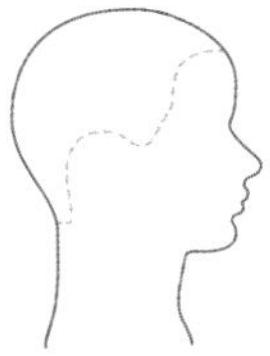

DESIGN PRINCIPLE

☐ ☐ ☐ ☐

SECTION/PART

APPLY

☐ ☐ ☐ ☐ ☐ ☐ ☐

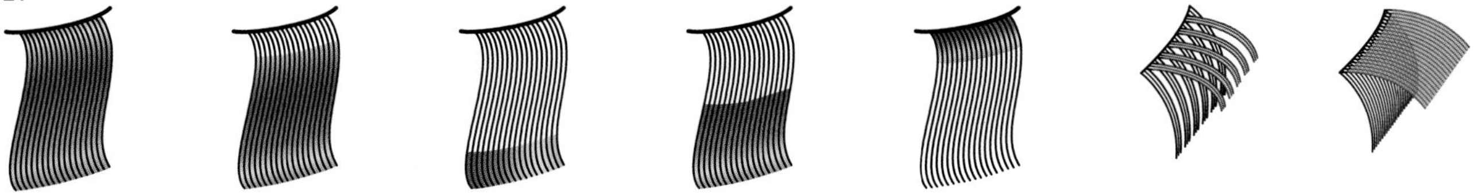

TOOLS

____

____

____

____

PRODUCT FORMULA/MIXING RATIO

COLORING/LIGHTENING PRODUCT ____________________

DEVELOPER/PEROXIDE STRENGTH ____________________

COLOR REFRESHER (IF APPLICABLE) ____________________

PROCESSING TIME ____________________

Instructor Signature ____________________ **Date** __________

SEMI-PERMANENT

View the video, complete the Design Decisions chart, then perform this workshop. Complete the self-check as you progress through the workshop.

10 mins
Suggested
Salon Speed

PREPARATION	✔
>> Assemble tools and products >> Set up workstation >> Workshop is performed on uniform lengths	☐

SECTION

1. **Section hair into 4 areas:**
   >> Center front hairline to nape
   >> Apex to top of each ear   ☐

2. **Position head upright.**   ☐

3. **Apply barrier cream to skin around hairline for protection:**
   >> Wear gloves   ☐

PART/APPLY – BASE/MIDSTRAND

4. **Apply color using applicator bottle:**
   >> Outline sectioning lines in back
   >> 1" (2.5 cm) horizontal partings
   >> Work from top to nape
   >> Apply base-to-midstrand, omitting porous ends
   >> Work to nape
   >> Repeat on opposite back section   ☐

5. **Apply color to sides:**
   >> Outline sections
   >> Diagonal partings
   >> Apply base-to-midstrand
   >> Work from top to front hairline
   >> Apply along hairline   ☐

APPLY — MIDSTRAND AND ENDS ✔

6. **Apply color to midstrand and ends:**
   - » Horizontal partings in back
   - » Diagonal-back partings at sides
   - » Work from top to bottom
   - » Work color through for even saturation

☐

PROCESS/TEST/REMOVE AND CONDITION

7. **Process color and strand test:**
   - » Apply cotton around hairline
   - » Place plastic cap over hair
   - » Process color according to manufacturer's instructions
   - » Perform strand test to check color
   - » Follow manufacturer's instructions for removing and conditioning

☐

8. **The finish shows a tonal change to a warm red shade with enhanced shine.**

☐

COMPLETION

   - » Discard single-use supplies
   - » Disinfect tools and multi-use supplies
   - » Disinfect workstation and arrange in proper order

☐

10 mins
Suggested Salon Speed

My Speed
———
———
———

INSTRUCTIONS:
Record your time in comparison with the suggested salon speed. Then, list here how you could improve your performance.

_____
_____
_____
_____
_____

VIRGIN DARKER

EXPLORE:

Have you ever noticed your mood change when you're in a solid dark room as opposed to a light or multi-colored room?

INSPIRE:

Mastering the virgin darker color application is crucial to being successful in the salon today, as its fundamental skills are required for most color application patterns and techniques.

ACHIEVE:

Following this *Virgin Darker Workshop*, you'll be able to:

>> Identify the color procedures related to the virgin darker technique

>> Apply color neatly and evenly from base to ends

>> Create a repetition of color that allows maximum light reflection

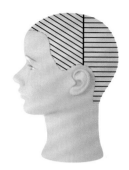

An even, darker color applied all over will enhance the sleek, smooth look of this solid form.

A repetition of color is applied to the entire head using horizontal partings in the back and diagonal-back partings at the sides.

COLOR DESIGN PROCEDURES

1. SECTION: 4 sections

2. PART:
   Back – Horizontal | Sides – Diagonal back

3. APPLY:
   Base to ends

4. PROCESS:
   Manufacturer's instructions

5 . TEST: Strand test

6. REMOVE AND CONDITION:
   Manufacturer's instructions

DESIGN DECISIONS CHART

VIRGIN DARKER

Draw or fill in the boxes with the appropriate answers.

DESIGN DECISIONS

EXISTING/DESIRED LEVEL

E E E E E

D D D D D

FORM/TEXTURE

DESIGN PRINCIPLE

☐ ☐ ☐ ☐

PATTERN/SECTION/PART

TOP	RIGHT	LEFT	BACK

APPLY

☐ ☐ ☐ ☐ ☐ ☐ ☐

TOOLS

_____

_____

_____

_____

PRODUCT FORMULA/MIXING RATIO

COLORING/LIGHTENING PRODUCT_____

DEVELOPER/PEROXIDE STRENGTH _____

COLOR REFRESHER (IF APPLICABLE) _____

PROCESSING TIME _____

Instructor Signature _____ **Date** _____

VIRGIN DARKER

View the video, complete the Design Decisions chart, then perform this workshop. Complete the self-check as you progress through the workshop.

15 mins
Suggested
Salon Speed

PREPARATION	✔
>> Assemble tools and products >> Set up workstation >> Workshop is performed on solid lengths	☐

SECTION	
1. Section hair into 4 areas: >> Center front hairline to center back >> Top of head to each ear	☐
2. Position head upright.	☐
3. Apply barrier cream around hairline: >> Wear gloves	☐

PART/APPLY — BACK	
4. Apply color using the virgin darker technique: >> Part ¼" (.6 cm) parting horizontally across nape >> Apply color neatly and evenly from base to ends >> Work product through hair with thumb and fingers	☐

5. **Work upward toward crown using same procedures:**
   - » Subdivide ¼" (.6 cm) partings for control

6. **Apply generous amount of product to hair:**
   - » Comb through back sections to ensure even coverage

PART/APPLY – SIDES

7. **Apply color to left side:**
   - » ¼" (.6 cm) diagonal-back parting at top of left side
   - » Apply color neatly and evenly from base to ends
   - » Lay hair away from face
   - » Work downward using same technique
   - » Subdivide wider partings for control

8. **Apply color to right side:**
   - » Repeat same procedure on opposite side
   - » Avoid product seepage onto skin
   - » Outline hairline to ensure coverage
   - » Comb hair away from face to ensure even distribution

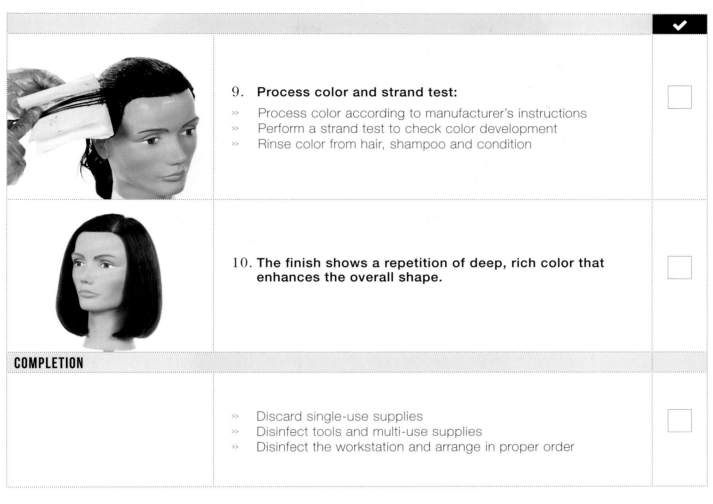

9. **Process color and strand test:**
   >> Process color according to manufacturer's instructions
   >> Perform a strand test to check color development
   >> Rinse color from hair, shampoo and condition

10. **The finish shows a repetition of deep, rich color that enhances the overall shape.**

COMPLETION

>> Discard single-use supplies
>> Disinfect tools and multi-use supplies
>> Disinfect the workstation and arrange in proper order

15 mins
Suggested
Salon Speed

My Speed
———
———
———

INSTRUCTIONS:
Record your time in comparison with the suggested salon speed. Then, list here how you could improve your performance.

_____
_____
_____
_____
_____

VARIATION – VIRGIN DARKER

A variation on the virgin darker technique using a bottle application is available online.

RETOUCH/REFRESH

EXPLORE

How would you preserve the health of your clients' hair when they regularly visit you for retouch applications?

INSPIRE

Retouch applications are a fundamental hair color service and are performed every 3-6 weeks. Adding a refresh to midlengths and ends adds shine and boosts color vitality.

ACHIEVE

Following this *Retouch/Refresh Workshop*, you'll be able to:

>> Identify the color procedures related to retouch/refresh applications

>> Apply permanent color neatly to the regrowth

>> Apply demi-permanent color neatly to the midstrand and ends

>> Demonstrate proper procedures to create a consistent color result, while touching up regrowth and refreshing lengths with a different color product

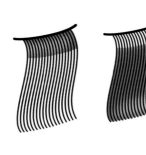
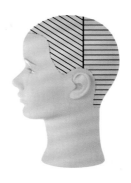
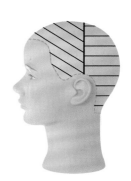

An overall rich color is achieved during a retouch service using permanent color at the base and demi-permanent color of the same shade through the lengths.

A bowl-and-brush application is used for the retouch, and a bottle application is used to refresh the lengths.

COLOR DESIGN PROCEDURES

RETOUCH   REFRESH

1. SECTION: 4 sections

2. PART:
   Back – Horizontal | Sides – Diagonal back

3. APPLY:
   Retouch – Base | Refresh – Midstrand to ends

4. PROCESS:
   Manufacturer's instructions

5. TEST: Strand test

6. REMOVE AND CONDITION:
   Manufacturer's instructions

DESIGN DECISIONS CHART

RETOUCH/REFRESH

Draw or fill in the boxes with the appropriate answers.

DESIGN DECISIONS

EXISTING/DESIRED LEVEL

E   E   E   E   E

D   D   D   D   D

FORM/TEXTURE

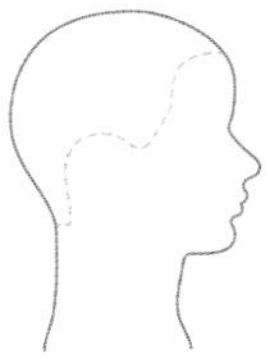

DESIGN PRINCIPLE

☐   ☐   ☐   ☐

SECTION/PART

RETOUCH   RETOUCH 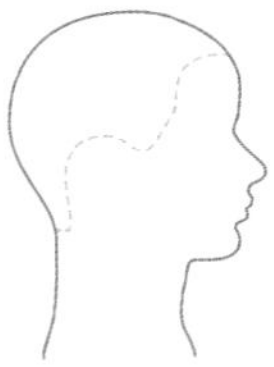   REFRESH 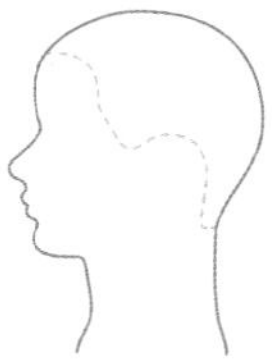   REFRESH

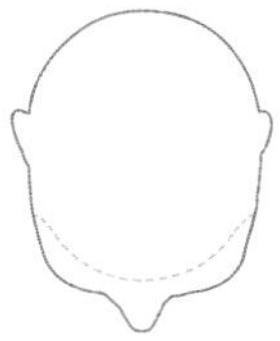

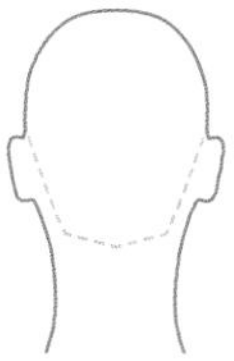

APPLY

☐   ☐   ☐   ☐   ☐   ☐   ☐

TOOLS

_____

_____

_____

_____

PRODUCT FORMULA/MIXING RATIO

COLORING/LIGHTENING PRODUCT _____

DEVELOPER/PEROXIDE STRENGTH _____

COLOR REFRESHER (IF APPLICABLE) _____

PROCESSING TIME _____

Instructor Signature _____ **Date** _____

RETOUCH/REFRESH

View the video, complete the Design Decisions chart, then perform this workshop. Complete the self-check as you progress through the workshop.

20 mins
Suggested
Salon Speed

PREPARATION	✔
>> Assemble tools and products >> Set up workstation >> Workshop is performed on short, graduated lengths >> Drape client for chemical service	☐

SECTION

1. **Section hair into 4 areas:**
   - >> Center-front hairline to nape
   - >> Behind apex to each ear

   ☐

2. **Protect hairline and skin:**
   - >> Wear gloves
   - >> Apply barrier cream around hairline and ears

   ☐

PART/APPLY – REGROWTH

3. **Apply permanent color to regrowth:**
   - >> Outline sectioning lines in back
   - >> ¼" (.6 cm) horizontal partings at top
   - >> Load color brush with even amount of color
   - >> Apply to regrowth only
   - >> Apply on both top and bottom of parting
   - >> Lay hair up and over

   ☐

4. **Work downward from crown to nape:**

>> Do not overlap product on previously colored hair
>> Subdivide partings for control
>> Keep laying hair up and over loosely
>> Complete regrowth application in nape
>> Bring section down to promote oxidation
>> Repeat on opposite back section

5. **Use same base application technique on sides:**

>> Outline front section
>> Begin at top of section, near crown
>> ¼" (.6 cm) diagonal-back partings
>> Continue to apply color only to regrowth
>> Subdivide partings for control
>> Work to bottom of section
>> Repeat on opposite side

6. **Carefully apply along hairline without staining the skin:**

>> Bring each section down to promote oxidation

PART/APPLY – MIDSTRAND AND ENDS

7. **Apply a refresh color to midstrand and ends:**

>> Mix demi-permanent color product of matching shade in applicator bottle
>> Begin at crown in back section
>> Take a ½" (1.25 cm) horizontal parting away from base
>> Apply color to midlength and ends
>> Work from top of section to bottom
>> Use your thumb and fingers to work product through hair and ensure coverage
>> Bring hair down to allow oxidation

8. **Repeat on opposite back section.**

	✔

9. Apply refresh color to side sections:
>> Begin in top of section
>> Diagonal-back partings
>> Apply color with same technique
>> Direct hair back and away from face

☐

PROCESS/TEST/REMOVE AND CONDITION

10. Process color and strand test:
>> Clean around hairline to avoid staining skin
>> Process color according to manufacturer's instructions
>> Perform strand test to check color development
>> Rinse color from hair, shampoo and condition

☐

11. The finish shows a rich color. The refresh color adds shine, brightness and vibrancy to the existing lighter strands, creating a soft, multidimensional look.

☐

COMPLETION

>> Discard single-use supplies
>> Disinfect tools and multi-use supplies
>> Disinfect workstation and arrange in proper order

☐

20 mins
Suggested Salon Speed

My Speed
_____
_____
_____

INSTRUCTIONS:
Record your time in comparison with the suggested salon speed. Then, list here how you could improve your performance.

_____

_____

_____

_____

_____

PARTIAL HIGHLIGHTS/SLICING

EXPLORE

Have you or someone you know ever had a little hair color added just for interest to the overall look?

INSPIRE

Many clients will initially shy away from full highlights and instead opt for a more low-maintenance, partial highlight service to brighten their features and add interest to their hairstyles.

ACHIEVE

Following this *Partial Highlights/Slicing Workshop*, you'll be able to:

» Identify the color procedures related to Partial Highlights/Slicing technique

» Demonstrate proper procedures to achieve partial highlights using a slicing technique

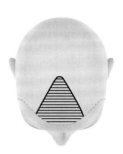

Partial highlights in the fringe area add softness and dimension around the face.

A light warm blond is introduced to this medium-dark field with fine horizontal slices within a triangle shape, positioned at the fringe area.

COLOR DESIGN PROCEDURES

1. SECTION: Triangle

2. PART: Horizontal

3. APPLY: Base to ends

4. PROCESS: Manufacturer's instructions

5. TEST: Strand test

6. REMOVE AND CONDITION: Manufacturer's instructions

DESIGN DECISIONS CHART
PARTIAL HIGHLIGHTS/SLICING
Draw or fill in the boxes with the appropriate answers.

DESIGN DECISIONS

EXISTING/DESIRED LEVEL

E	E	E	E	E
D	D	D	D	D

FORM/TEXTURE

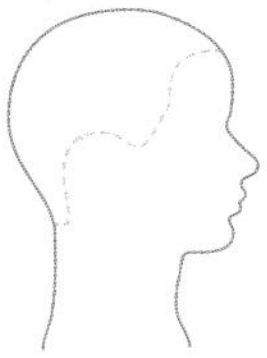

DESIGN PRINCIPLE

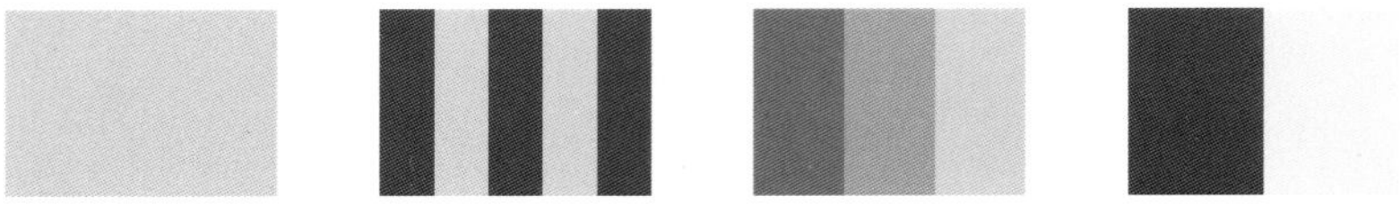

☐ ☐ ☐ ☐

SECTION/PART

APPLY

☐ ☐ ☐ ☐ ☐ ☐ ☐

TOOLS

_____
_____
_____
_____

PRODUCT FORMULA/MIXING RATIO

COLORING/LIGHTENING PRODUCT _____

DEVELOPER/PEROXIDE STRENGTH _____

COLOR REFRESHER (IF APPLICABLE) _____

PROCESSING TIME _____

Instructor Signature _____ **Date** _____

PARTIAL HIGHLIGHTS/SLICING

View the video, complete the Design Decisions chart, and then perform this workshop. Complete the self-check as you progress through the workshop.

15 mins
Suggested
Salon Speed

PREPARATION	✔
>> Assemble tools and products >> Set up workstation >> Workshop is performed on graduated lengths	☐

SECTION

	1. **Section triangle at fringe:** >> Use tail comb >> Section from above center of eyes to apex >> Secure remainder of hair out of way	☐
	2. **Mix lightener:** >> Follow manufacturer's instructions >> Wear gloves	☐

PART/APPLY

	3. **Use slicing technique:** >> ½" (1.25 cm) horizontal partings >> Part fine slice from top of parting >> Leave front hairline natural and double the density of fine slice	☐

4. **Apply lightener away from base to ends:**

>> Position foil underneath strand
>> Position brush on angle
>> Apply in zigzag pattern near edge of foil
>> For midstrand and ends application, position hand underneath foil
>> Apply lightener through ends

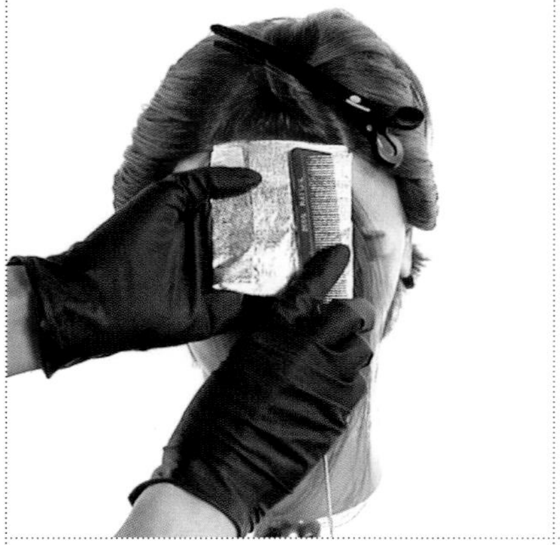

5. **Close foil neatly:**

>> Fold foil upward in half
>> Avoid pulling foil away from base
>> Fold sides of foil toward center with tail comb

6. **Work toward narrow end of triangle using the same techniques:**

>> Apply product using same procedure
>> Fold foil using same technique

PROCESS/TEST/REMOVE AND CONDITION

7. **Process color:**

>> Carefully clip highlighted section up to protect eyes
>> Process color according to manufacturer's instructions
>> Strand test for desired degree of lightening
>> Remove foils
>> Rinse, shampoo and condition

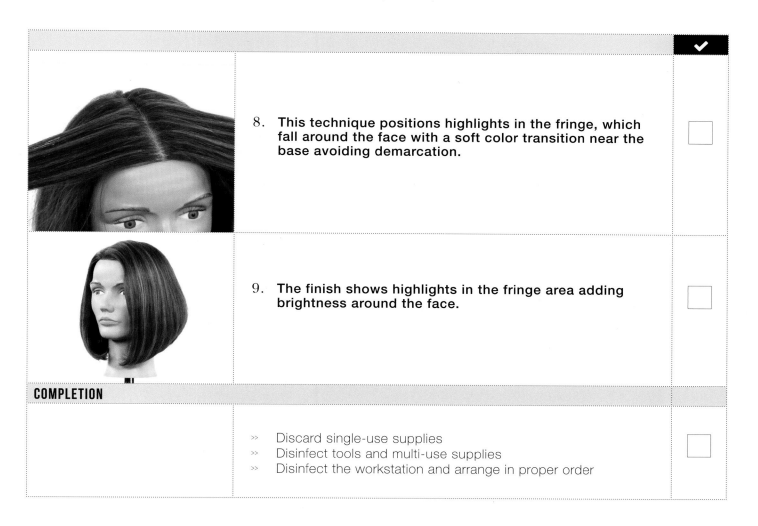

8. This technique positions highlights in the fringe, which fall around the face with a soft color transition near the base avoiding demarcation.

☐

9. The finish shows highlights in the fringe area adding brightness around the face.

☐

COMPLETION

>> Discard single-use supplies
>> Disinfect tools and multi-use supplies
>> Disinfect the workstation and arrange in proper order

☐

15 mins
Suggested Salon Speed

My Speed
_____
_____
_____

INSTRUCTIONS:

Record your time in comparison with the Suggested Salon Speed. Then, list here how you could improve your performance.

_____
_____
_____
_____
_____

VARIATION – PARTIAL HIGHLIGHTS/SLICING

A variation on the partial highlights/slicing technique is available online.

FREEHAND PAINTING

EXPLORE

Can you recall a time when you actually liked how a darker regrowth added dimension? Or when the ends of your hair were lightened by the sun?

INSPIRE

The soft, blended results of freehand painting are a great way to introduce clients to color. Freehand painting is a staple highlight service in the salon.

ACHIEVE

Following this *Freehand Painting Workshop,* you'll be able to:

>> Identify the color procedures related to freehand painting along the strand

>> Demonstrate proper procedures for the freehand painting color technique

>> Create a soft progression from a darker base to lighter ends

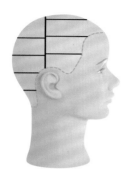

The result of this technique will be a subtle variegated progression of lighter tones toward the ends.

The freehand painting technique is performed using a horizontal parting pattern to create a subtle lightened effect along the midstrand and ends.

COLOR DESIGN PROCEDURES

1. SECTION: Ear to ear

2. PART: Horizontal

3. APPLY:
   Midstrand to ends

4. PROCESS:
   Manufacturer's instructions

5. TEST: Strand test

6. REMOVE AND CONDITION:
   Manufacturer's instructions

DESIGN DECISIONS CHART
FREEHAND PAINTING
Draw or fill in the boxes with the appropriate answers.

DESIGN DECISIONS

EXISTING/DESIRED LEVEL

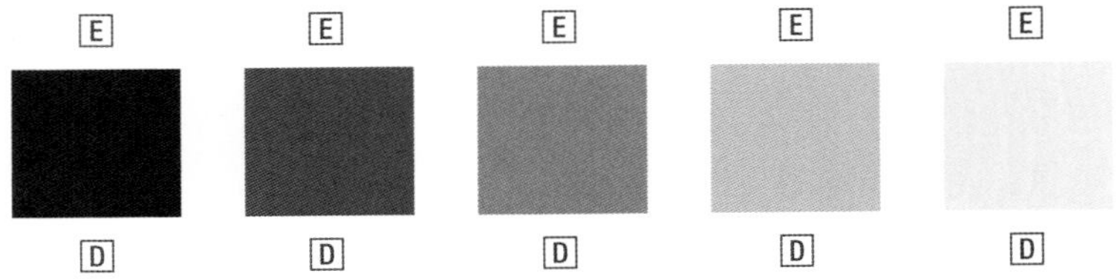

E E E E E

D D D D D

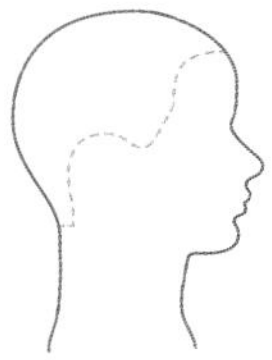

DESIGN PRINCIPLE

☐ ☐ ☐ ☐

FORM/TEXTURE

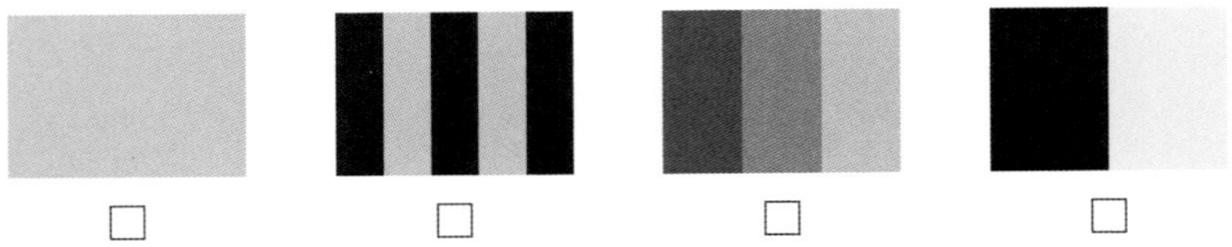

SECTION/PART

APPLY

☐ ☐ ☐ ☐ ☐ ☐ ☐

TOOLS

_____
_____
_____
_____

PRODUCT FORMULA/MIXING RATIO

COLORING/LIGHTENING PRODUCT _____

DEVELOPER/PEROXIDE STRENGTH _____

COLOR REFRESHER (IF APPLICABLE) _____

PROCESSING TIME _____

Instructor Signature _____ Date _____

FREEHAND PAINTING

View the video, complete the Design Decisions chart, then perform this workshop. Complete the self-check as you progress through the workshop.

15 mins
Suggested Salon Speed

PREPARATION	✔

>> Assemble tools and products
>> Set up workstation
>> Workshop is performed on increase-layered lengths

☐

SECTION

1. **Section from ear to ear:**

>> Apex to top of each ear
>> Off-center parting based on styling preference

☐

2. **Position head upright.**

☐

PART/APPLY — SIDES

3. **Apply lightener or color product with the freehand painting technique:**

>> Begin on heavier side
>> 2"-2½" (5-6.25 cm) horizontal partings
>> Position brush vertically
>> Apply product away from base through ends of selected strands
>> Start at varying points of strand for soft transition

☐

4. **Work toward top:**

>> Avoid shifting hair
>> Project parting slightly while applying
>> Subdivide wider partings for control
>> Leave hair near side part natural
>> Repeat on opposite side

☐

✓

5. **Apply to back using freehand painting technique:**
   - » Begin in nape
   - » 2"-2½" (5-6.25 cm) horizontal partings
   - » Subdivide for control

6. **Work toward top:**
   - » Leave interior surface hair natural
   - » Check to ensure a balanced product application pattern before processing

PROCESS/TEST/REMOVE AND CONDITION

7. **Process color:**
   - » Follow manufacturer's instructions
   - » Strand test for desired degree of lightening
   - » Rinse, shampoo and condition

8. **The finish shows subtle progression of lighter tones toward the ends that accentuate the texture of this layered look.**

COMPLETION

   - » Discard single-use supplies
   - » Disinfect tools and multi-use supplies
   - » Disinfect workstation and arrange in proper order

15 mins
Suggested Salon Speed

My Speed
_____
_____
_____

INSTRUCTIONS:
Record your time in comparison with the suggested salon speed. Then, list here how you could improve your performance.

_____
_____
_____
_____

ZONES

EXPLORE

Do you remember learning at some point in school that lighter colors stand out and darker colors recede? Do you think this principle applies to hair colors within zones?

INSPIRE

Zonal patterns are commonly used to create a progression of colors, which can create an illusion of added fullness and depth based on zone placement and color choices.

ACHIEVE

Following this *Zones Workshop*, you'll be able to:

>> Identify the color procedures related to the zones color technique

>> Demonstrate and perform proper techniques for a zonal color on the increase-layered form

>> Create a progression of colors resulting in the illusion of added depth and dimension

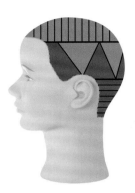

A progression of colors gradually gets lighter toward the top with more depth in the longer lengths.

Within three horizontal zones, the lightest color is applied in the top and the darkest is applied in the bottom zone. Alternating both colors in the middle zone allows for maximum blending between the interior and exterior.

COLOR DESIGN PROCEDURES

1. SECTION:
   3 horizontal sections | Middle section – Triangles

2. PART: Horizontal

3. APPLY:
   Base to ends

4. PROCESS:
   Manufacturer's instructions

5. TEST:
   Strand test

6. REMOVE AND CONDITION:
   Manufacturer's instructions

ZONES

Draw or fill in the boxes with the appropriate answers.

DESIGN DECISIONS

EXISTING/DESIRED LEVEL

E   E   E   E   E

D   D   D   D   D

FORM/TEXTURE

DESIGN PRINCIPLE

☐   ☐   ☐   ☐

SECTION/PART

APPLY

☐   ☐   ☐   ☐   ☐   ☐   ☐

TOOLS

_____

_____

_____

_____

PRODUCT FORMULA/MIXING RATIO

COLORING/LIGHTENING PRODUCT _____

DEVELOPER/PEROXIDE STRENGTH _____

COLOR REFRESHER (IF APPLICABLE) _____

PROCESSING TIME _____

Instructor Signature _____ **Date** _____

PERFORMANCE GUIDE

ZONES

View the video, complete the Design Decisions chart, then perform this workshop. Complete the self-check as you progress through the workshop.

35 mins
Suggested Salon Speed

PREPARATION	✔

>> Assemble tools and products >> Set up workstation >> Workshop is performed on increase-layered lengths	☐

SECTION	

1. **Section 3 zones:**
   - >> Horizontally at occipital and recession
   - >> Subsection middle zone with steep zigzag partings, resulting in 9 alternating triangles

   ☐

2. **Protect skin:**
   - >> Apply barrier cream around hairline
   - >> Wear gloves
   - >> Mix color product

   ☐

PART/APPLY — NAPE AND BACK	

3. **Apply color in bottom zone:**
   - >> ¼" (.6 cm) horizontal partings
   - >> Begin at center nape
   - >> Apply dark color to top and bottom of strand

   ☐

4. **Apply from base to ends, working to top of section.**

   ☐

5. **Apply dark color to alternating triangles:**
   >> Cover bottom section with long thermal strips
   >> Release triangles with wide end at bottom

6. **Start in center back:**
   >> Part horizontally
   >> Apply dark color from base to ends

7. **Work to top of triangle.**

8. **Outline section to ensure coverage.**

9. **Apply dark color to alternating triangles:**
   >> Work from one side then other side
   >> Place thermal strip underneath lengths at face

10. **Apply lighter color to remaining triangles:**
    >> Release remaining triangles in midsection
    >> Horizontal partings
    >> Apply lighter color from base to ends
    >> Outline section
    >> Work toward one side then other side
    >> Cover middle zone with long thermal strips

PART/APPLY – TOP

11. Apply lighter color to top section:

>> Begin at back of section
>> ¼" (.6 cm) horizontal partings
>> Subdivide partings for control

12. Work to front using consistent partings:

>> Apply color from base to ends
>> Direct partings away from face

13. Avoid staining skin in last parting.

14. Outline section to complete application.

PROCESS/TEST/REMOVE AND CONDITION ✔

15. **Process, strand test and remove color:**

    >> Set timer according to manufacturer's instructions
    >> Perform strand test
    >> Rinse, shampoo and condition hair

    ☐

16. **The finish shows a blend of colors, creating a soft progression from the interior to the exterior.**

    ☐

COMPLETION

>> Discard single-use supplies
>> Disinfect tools and multi-use supplies
>> Disinfect the workstation and arrange in proper order

☐

35 mins
Suggested Salon Speed

My Speed
_____
_____
_____

INSTRUCTIONS:
Record your time in comparison with the suggested salon speed. Then, list here how you could improve your performance.

_____
_____
_____
_____
_____

FULL HEAD HIGHLIGHTS

EXPLORE

How do you think highlights might affect the way you perceive the texture within a hairstyle?

INSPIRE

Mastering the classic highlighting technique is the foundation for a large range of professional color services.

ACHIEVE

Following this *Full Head Highlights Workshop*, you'll be able to:

>> Identify the color procedures related to full head highlights

>> Demonstrate proper procedures to achieve highlights using a weaving technique

>> Create a fine alternation of lighter and darker colors within a uniform hairstyle

A multidimensional color effect enhances the layered texture of the style.

Woven highlights created with horizontal and diagonal-back partings result in a color alternation throughout.

COLOR DESIGN PROCEDURES

1. SECTION: 4 sections

2. PART:
   Back – Horizontal | Sides – Diagonal

3. APPLY: Base to ends

4. PROCESS:
   Manufacturer's instructions

5. TEST: Strand test

6. REMOVE AND CONDITION:
   Manufacturer's instructions

DESIGN DECISIONS CHART

FULL HEAD HIGHLIGHTS

Draw or fill in the boxes with the appropriate answers.

DESIGN DECISIONS

EXISTING/DESIRED LEVEL

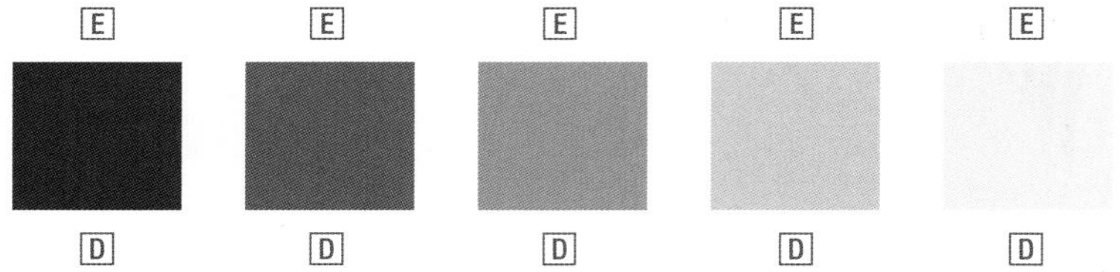

E E E E E

D D D D D

FORM/TEXTURE

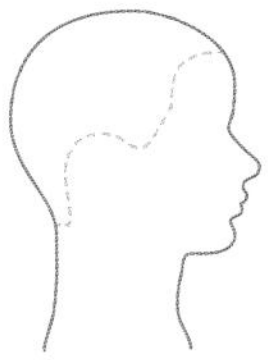

DESIGN PRINCIPLE

☐ ☐ ☐ ☐

SECTION/PART

APPLY

☐ ☐ ☐ ☐ ☐ ☐ ☐

TOOLS

_____

_____

_____

_____

PRODUCT FORMULA/MIXING RATIO

COLORING/LIGHTENING PRODUCT _____

DEVELOPER/PEROXIDE STRENGTH _____

COLOR REFRESHER (IF APPLICABLE) _____

PROCESSING TIME _____

Instructor Signature _____ **Date** _____

FULL HEAD HIGHLIGHTS

View the video, complete the Design Decisions chart, then perform this workshop. Complete the self-check as you progress through the workshop.

45 mins
Suggested
Salon Speed

PREPARATION	✔
>> Assemble tools and products >> Set up workstation >> Workshop is performed on uniform lengths	☐

SECTION	
1. Section hair into 4 areas: >> Center-front hairline to nape >> Apex to top of each ear	☐
2. Protect skin: >> Wear gloves	☐

PART/APPLY — BACK	
3. Create highlight weaves in the nape: >> Mix lower strength developer with powder lightener >> Part horizontally along nape hairline >> On one side create a fine weave from top of parting using tail comb >> Position pre-folded edge of foil underneath weaves using tail of metal tail comb	☐
4. Apply lightener in foil: >> Pick up even amount of lightener on ends of color brush >> Hold brush parallel to parting and apply lightener from edge of foil to ends	☐

5. **Close foil with double-fold technique:**

>> Fold bottom third of foil upward to about halfway along strand

>> Fold foil once more to edge of base

>> Fold sides inward
>> Repeat on other side of nape

6. **Create a bricklay pattern, working up back:**
>> Release medium-fine horizontal parting across back
>> Subdivide wider partings when needed
>> Use same weaving and foiling technique
>> Work from center to one side, then to other side

PART/APPLY – SIDES

7. **Place highlights in sides working from bottom to top:**
>> Mix higher strength developer with powder lightener
>> Take medium-fine diagonal-back partings
>> Use same weaving and foiling technique
>> Work from hairline to the top

8. **Work toward top:**

>> Subdivide partings when needed

9. **Complete other side with same techniques.**

PROCESS/TEST/REMOVE

10. **Process and strand test for desired degree of lightness:**

>> Set a timer according to manufacturer's instructions
>> Take strand test
>> Remove foils
>> Rinse, shampoo and dry hair

PART/APPLY – TONER

11. **Neutralize warm tones:**

>> Mix toner color with catalyst (processing lotion)
>> Section 4 sections
>> ½" (1.25 cm) diagonal-back partings at sides; horizontal partings in back
>> Apply from base to ends
>> Work from top to bottom of each section
>> Distribute evenly throughout

PROCESS/TEST/REMOVE AND CONDITION ✔

12. Process toner and strand test:

» Process according to manufacturer's instructions
» Rinse, shampoo and condition

☐

13. The finish shows a harmonious blend of lightened and darker natural hair that adds dimension and creates the illusion of greater textural activation.

☐

COMPLETION

» Discard single-use supplies
» Disinfect tools and multi-use supplies
» Disinfect the workstation and arrange in proper order

☐

45 mins
Suggested
Salon Speed

My Speed
_____
_____
_____

INSTRUCTIONS:
Record your time in comparison with the suggested salon speed. Then, list here how you could improve your performance.

_____
_____
_____
_____
_____

VARIATION – FULL HEAD HIGHLIGHTS/LOWLIGHTS

A variation on the full head highlights/lowlights technique is available online.

VIRGIN LIGHTER

EXPLORE

There's an old saying that goes: "Blondes have more fun." Would you agree? Where might this saying come from?

INSPIRE

Mastering this challenging double-process technique will give you an elevated skill and a loyal blond service clientele. It also serves as the foundation for creating trendy, bright fashion colors at professional salon quality.

ACHIEVE

Following this *Virgin Lighter Workshop*, you'll be able to:

>> Identify the color procedures related to the double-process blond color technique

>> Demonstrate proper decolorization procedures

>> Demonstrate proper recolorization procedures

>> Create a repetition of light blond color

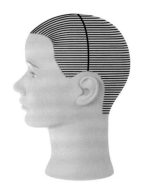

The finish shows a light beige blond created by first lightening and then toning the hair, also referred to as a double-process blond technique.

A repetition of blond color is achieved throughout the entire head with the initial decolorization done with ⅛" (.3 cm) partings, followed by recolorization or toning done with ¼" (.6 cm) partings.

COLOR DESIGN PROCEDURES

1. SECTION: 4 Sections

2. PART:
   Decolorization: Horizontal

   Recolorization:
   Back – Horizontal
   Sides – Diagonal

3. APPLY:
   Decolorization – Midstrand to ends, then base

   Recolorization – Base to ends

4. PROCESS:
   Manufacturer's instructions

5. TEST: Strand test

6. REMOVE AND CONDITION:
   Manufacturer's instructions

VIRGIN LIGHTER

Draw or fill in the boxes with the appropriate answers.

DESIGN DECISIONS

EXISTING/DESIRED LEVEL

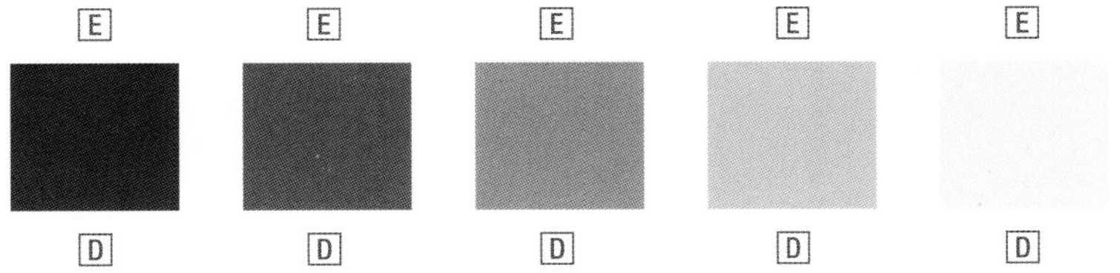

E E E E E

D D D D D

FORM/TEXTURE

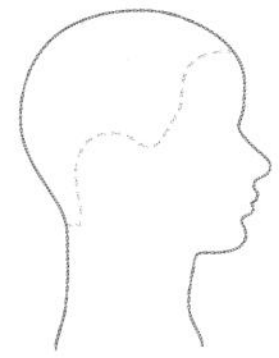

DESIGN PRINCIPLE

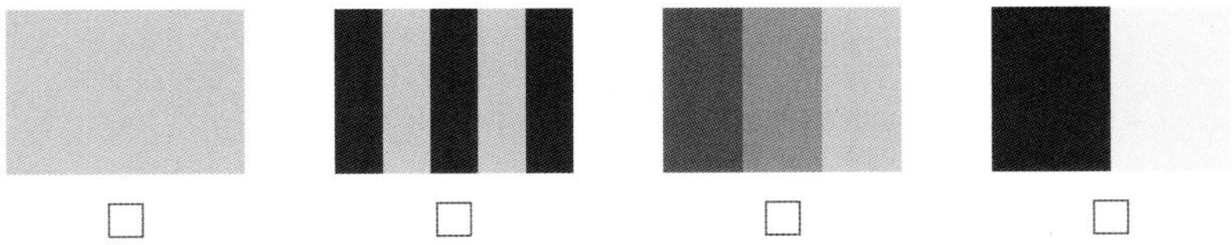

☐ ☐ ☐ ☐

SECTION/PART

APPLY

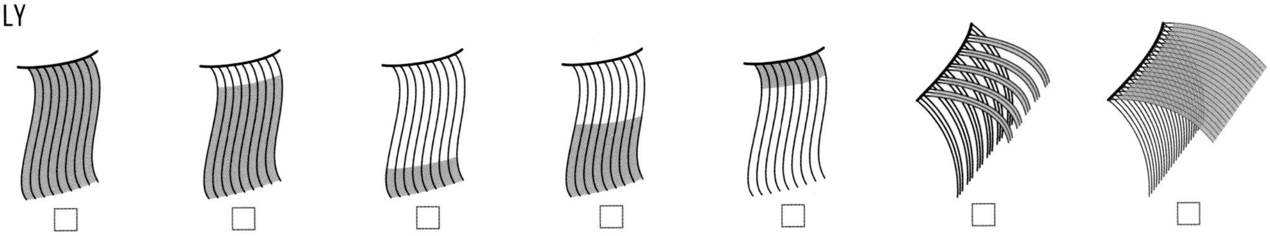

☐ ☐ ☐ ☐ ☐ ☐ ☐

TOOLS

_____

_____

_____

_____

PRODUCT FORMULA/MIXING RATIO

COLORING/LIGHTENING PRODUCT _____

DEVELOPER/PEROXIDE STRENGTH _____

COLOR REFRESHER (IF APPLICABLE) _____

PROCESSING TIME _____

Instructor Signature _____ Date _____

PERFORMANCE GUIDE

VIRGIN LIGHTER

View the video, complete the Design Decisions chart, then perform this workshop. Complete the self-check as you progress through the workshop.

35 mins
Suggested
Salon Speed*

PREPARATION ✓

>> Assemble tools and products
>> Set up workstation
>> Workshop is performed on graduated/uniform combination form

☐

SECTIONING

1. **Section hair into 4 areas:**

>> Center-front hairline to nape
>> Apex to top of each ear

☐

2. **Protect hairline and skin:**

>> Wear gloves
>> Apply barrier cream around hairline

☐

PART/APPLY – NAPE AND BACK

3. **Apply lightener in back section away from scalp to ends:**

>> ⅛" (.3 cm) horizontal partings
>> Place cotton under strand
>> Apply lightener ½" (1.25 cm) away from scalp through to ends

☐

4. **Place cotton at base, in between partings, to prevent seepage.**

☐

*15 mins, midstrand, ends; 10 mins, base; 10 mins, toner

5. Work upward to complete back section:

>> Repeat same procedures
>> Place cotton at base as you work up head

☐

6. Repeat on other back section.

☐

APPLY – SIDES

7. Move to sides and use same procedures.

>> Horizontal partings
>> Begin at bottom of side section
>> Apply product on top and bottom of strand ½" (1.25 cm) away from base
>> Place cotton at base

☐

8. Work toward center top of head.

☐

9. Repeat on opposite side section.

☐

PROCESS/TEST

10. Process halfway to desired degree of lightness:

>> Set timer according to manufacturer's directions

☐

	✔
11. **Perform strand test to see if appropriate degree of lightness has been achieved.**	☐

APPLY – BASE

12. **Apply newly mixed lightener to base only:** >> Begin at top of back sections >> Remove cotton as you go	☐
13. **Complete back sections.**	☐

14. **Repeat on side sections.** ☐

15. **Outline each section to ensure even coverage:**
>> Bring each section down to promote oxidation ☐

PROCESS/TEST/REMOVE

16. **Strand test periodically:**
>> Check that desired degree of lightness has been achieved
>> Rinse hair with cool water, gently shampoo and towel-dry
>> Re-examine scalp for abrasions and any irritations ☐

PART/APPLY — TONER ✓

17. Apply toner through hair and process:

>> Mix toner in applicator bottle
>> ¼" (.6 cm) diagonal-back partings at sides and horizontal partings in back
>> Perform strand test for color development
>> Rinse, shampoo and condition hair

☐

18. The finish shows a beautiful, light-beige blond with even and consistent color throughout.

☐

COMPLETION

>> Discard single-use supplies
>> Disinfect tools and multi-use supplies
>> Disinfect workstation and arrange in proper order

☐

3.5 mins
Suggested Salon Speed

My Speed
———
———
———

INSTRUCTIONS:

Record your time in comparison with the suggested salon speed. Then, list here how you could improve your performance.

_____

_____

_____

_____

_____

NOTE

>> The area along the hairstrand where two colors meet (i.e., the area where the new growth meets the previously colored hair) is known as the **line of demarcation**. It is important to avoid overlapping the product, especially with a lightener retouch service, since it could cause breakage.

110^c GLOSSARY/INDEX

Drabber *64*
Product used to neutralize tones from the contributing pigment.

Draping *109*
Procedure used to protect client's skin and clothing.

Dye Solvent *59*
Products often known as color removers; designed to remove unwanted artificial pigment from the hair.

End Lights *90*
Dimensional color technique that lightens only the ends of the hair.

Eumelanin *35*
Type of melanin; (black pigment); a dense concentration will produce very dark hair; a small concentration will produce light (blond) hair.

Existing Color *32*
The color(s) present in the hair prior to the color design service; determines underlying pigment.

Fields of Color *59*
Categories of color; light, medium and dark; further divided into medium light and medium dark.

Filler *64*
Product that provides an even base color by filling in porous, damaged or abused areas with materials, such as protein or polymers; equalizes the porosity of the hair and deposits a base color in one application.

Foiling *76*
A method of highlighting or lowlighting, using foil to isolate the strands of hair to be lightened, colored or protected with conditioner.

Freeform Painting *89*
Technique in which a brush is used to strategically position color or lightener on parts of the hair.

Gray Hair *36*
Hair color caused by reduced color pigment in the cortex layer of the hair; heredity is the primary factor.

Henna *52*
Most common vegetable dye; natural color product that produces reddish hues and highlights in the hair.

High-Lift Tint *60*
Color with the ability to lift natural melanin 3-5 levels and deposit delicate tones; single-process color with a higher degree of lightening action and minimum amount of color deposit.

Highlighting *85*
A technique by which selected woven or sliced strands of hair are lightened.

Hue *8*
Name of a color, also referred to as tone, tells the warmth or coolness of a color; identified by its position on the color wheel.

Hydrogen Peroxide *61*
Most often used oxidizing or developing agent; H_2O_2.

Hydrometer *61*
Implement used to measure the strength (volume) of hydrogen peroxide.

Intensifier *64*
Undiluted color that can be added to any oxidative or nonoxidative color to enrich, or intensify, or occasionally tone down a color.

Intensity *16*
Refers to the vividness, brightness or saturation of a color within its own level; strength of the tone.

Keratin *35*
A protein that accounts for 97% of the makeup of hair.

Keratinization *124*
The process whereby cells change their shape, dry out and form keratin protein; once keratinized, the cells that form the hair fiber or strand are no longer alive.

Law of Color *7*
Of all the colors in the universe, only three—yellow, red and blue, called primary colors—are pure; these three primary colors create all other colors.

Level *13*
Also known as value or depth; the degree of lightness or darkness of a hair color relative to itself and others.

Lighteners *65*
Product used to decolorize, remove or diffuse pigment; utilizes ingredients, such as ammonia and peroxide, to facilitate the oxidation process.

Line of Demarcation *51*
An obvious difference between two colors along the hairstrand; can be a result of new growth or overlapping product onto previously color-treated hair.

Long-Lasting Semi-Permanent Hair Color *59*
Often referred to as demi-permanent color; generally does not contain ammonia; deposit-only colors.

Lowlighting *85*
A technique by which selected woven or sliced strands of hair are darkened.

Medulla *35*
Central core of the hair shaft (often absent in fine or very fine hair).

Melanin *35*
Pigment that gives skin and hair their color.

Melanocytes *35*
Pigment-producing cells that exist among the dividing cells within the hair bulb.

Melanosomes *35*
Bundles of melanocytes that rest near the hair bulb's nourishment center, the dermal papilla.

Metallic Dye *53*
Hair dye containing metals; also known as progressive dye.

Neutral Colors *10*
Colors that contain all three primary colors (yellow, red and blue); neither warm nor cool tones are exhibited.

Nonoxidative color *48*
Hair color that adds pigment but does not lighten the existing hair color.

Oil Lightener *65*
Color product that uses a certain amount of ammonia to give high lift; mild form of lightener that can be used directly on the scalp.

On-the-Scalp Lightener *65*
Color product used to lighten the hair; when applied to the hair can touch the scalp without harm; available as oil or cream.

Oxidation *65*
Process of combining oxygen with other chemical ingredients.

Oxidative Colors *58*
Hair colors that need to be mixed with developers (oxidants); deposit color, or lift (lighten) and deposit color in a single-color process.

Part *87*
To create lines that subdivide shapes or sections of hair for better control and accuracy while applying color.

Patch Test *109*
A test used to see if a client has a negative or positive allergic reaction to a chemical product; required 24-48 hours prior to aniline derivative tints.

PIVOT POINT

 ACKNOWLEDGMENTS

Pivot Point Fundamental is designed to provide education to undergraduate students to help prepare them for licensure and an entry-level position in the cosmetology field. An undertaking of this magnitude requires the expertise and cooperation of many people who are experts in their field. Pivot Point takes pride in our internal team of educators who develop cosmetology, esthetics and nails education, along with our print and digital experts, designers, editors, illustrators and video producers. Pivot Point would like to express our many thanks to these talented individuals who have devoted themselves to the business of beauty, lifelong learning and especially for help raising the bar for future professionals in our industry.

EDUCATION DEVELOPMENT — **Janet Fisher // Sabine Held-Perez // Vasiliki A. Stavrakis**
Markel Artwell
Eileen Dubelbeis
Brian Fallon
Melissa Holmes
Lisa Luppino
Paul Suttles
Amy Gallagher
Lisa Kersting
Jamie Nabielec
Vic Piccolotto
Ericka Thelin
Jane Wegner

EDITORIAL — **Maureen Spurr // Wm. Bullion // Deidre Glover**
Liz Bagby
Jack Bernin
Lori Chapman

DESIGN & PRODUCTION — **Jennifer Eckstein // Rick Russell // Danya Shaikh**
Joanna Jakubowicz
Denise Podlin
Annette Baase
Agnieszka Hansen
Kristine Palmer
Tiffany Wu

PROJECT MANAGEMENT — **Jenny Allen // Ken Wegrzyn**

DIGITAL DEVELOPMENT — John Bernin
Javed Fouch
Anna Fehr
Matt McCarthy
Marcia Noriega
Corey Passage
Herb Potzus

Pivot Point also wishes to take this opportunity to acknowledge the many contributors and product concept testers who helped make this program possible.

INDUSTRY CONTRIBUTORS

Linda Burmeister
Esthetics

Jeanne Braa Foster
Dr. Dean Foster
Eyes on Cancer

Mandy Gross
Nails

Andrea D. Kelly, MA, MSW
University of Delaware

Rosanne Kinley
Infection Control
National Interstate Council

Lynn Maestro
Cirépil by Perron Rigot, Paris

Andrzej Matracki
World and European
Men's Champion

MODERN SALON

Rachel Molepske
Look Good Feel Better, PBA
CUT IT OUT, PBA

Peggy Moon
Liaison to Regulatory and Testing

Robert Richards
Fashion Illustrations

Clif St. Germain, Ph.D
Educational Consultant

Andis Company

International Dermal Institute

HairUWear Inc.

Lock & Loaded Men's Grooming

PRODUCT CONCEPT TESTING

Central Carolina
Community College
Millington, North Carolina

Gateway Community Colleges
Phoenix, Arizona

MC College
Edmonton, Alberta

Metro Beauty Academy
Allentown, Pennsylvania

Rowan Cabarrus
Community College
Kannapolis, North Carolina

Sunstate Academy of
Cosmetology and Massage
Ft. Myers, Florida

The Salon Professional Academy
Kokomo, Indiana

TONI&GUY Hairdressing Academy
Costa Mesa, California
Plano, Texas

Xenon Academy
Omaha, NE
Grand Island, NE

LEADERSHIP TEAM

Robert Passage
Chairman and CEO

Robert J. Sieh
Senior Vice President,
Finance and Operations

Judy Rambert
Vice President, Education

Kevin Cameron
Senior Vice President,
Education and Marketing

R.W. Miller
Vice President, Domestic Sales
and Field Education

Jan Laan
Vice President, International
Business Development

Katy O'Mahony
Director, Human Resources

In addition, we give special thanks to the North American Regulating agencies whose careful work protects us as well as our clients, enhancing the high quality of our work. These agencies include Occupational Health and Safety Agency (OSHA) and the U.S. Environmental Protection Agency (EPA). *Pivot Point Fundamentals*™ promotes use of their policies and procedures.

Pivot Point International would like to express our SPECIAL THANKS to the inspired visual artisans of Creative Commons, without whose talents this book of beauty would not be possible.